# MY EIGHT PRESIDENTS

★★★

# MY EIGHT PRESIDENTS

*Sarah McClendon*

WYDEN BOOKS

*Manufactured in the United States of America.*

FIRST EDITION

*Trade distribution by Simon and Schuster*
*A Division of Gulf + Western Corporation*
*New York, New York 10020*

*Designed by Tere LoPrete*

---

Library of Congress Cataloging in Publication Data

McClendon, Sarah.
    My eight presidents.

    Includes index.
    1. McClendon, Sarah. 2. Journalists—United States—Biography. 3. Presidents—United States. I. Title.
PN4874.M345A35    070.4'3'0924  [B]    78-3713
ISBN 0-88326-150-2

# Contents

Photo inserts follow pages 114 and 178

9-20-77

To Sarah Mc Clendon

Thank you for your thoughtful note.

Each time I've called on you at the press conferences you've asked superb questions.

Your friend,

Jimmy

**"THANK YOU, MR. PRESIDENT."** *I've always had lots of fan mail and hate mail, but it's good to have a pat from a friend like Jimmy Carter.*

Sarah:

I would not want to comment on the syntax and sentence structure of your column in the El Paso Times.

But I will say that the girl they used as your stand-in for the photograph is a pip of a woman.

Indeed she is — verily

JFK

**"A PIP."** *John F. Kennedy had an eye for women, so naturally my vanity got a lift out of this note.*

LYNDON B. JOHNSON
TEXAS

## United States Senate
### Office of the Democratic Leader
### Washington, D. C.

July 10, 1959

Dear Sarah:

I'm just real proud of your Texas enterprise, honey,
and awfully pleased that you took the time to write me
a note telling how you scooped all those big-name, big-
shot newspapermen.  I told them on the Senate Floor
yesterday before the session started (I didn't see you
there, by the way) how a little Texas gal beat them on
that Kozlov story.

Keep up the good work.

Sincerely,

Lyndon B. Johnson

Mrs. Sarah McClendon
National Press Building
Washington, D. C.

**"WHEN HE WAS GOOD . . ."** *Lyndon B. Johnson could charm anybody out of anything, and this note proves it once again.*

# MY EIGHT
# PRESIDENTS

# I

## Roots of an Independent

Although I became known as one of the Washington press corps' most outspoken reporters, when I first started working as a newspaper reporter in Washington in 1944, I was too shy to ask President Roosevelt any questions at all. I felt uncomfortable and out of place at Roosevelt's press conferences, and I rarely attended. When I did go, the other reporters' questions made me realize how much I didn't know about politics and government.

As I learned more about my new beat, I became more confident. By the time Harry S. Truman was president, I attended his press conferences regularly and asked occasional questions. Truman answered them with kindness and humor. I was determined to speak out at President Eisenhower's first press conference, and though all the odds were against me—I was standing in the balcony, far from the president, who read a long statement and thus left very little time for reporters' questions that day—it was that long statement which prompted my question and got an answer. Once I saw that I could participate, that my questions could make a difference, I kept asking Ike questions, to the point that people started blaming me for his high blood pressure. For a time, President Kennedy tried to avoid my questions completely. But he was too curious, and ended up calling on me at his press conferences just to see what I'd ask next. My questions made President Johnson squirm, and he lectured me about them, both privately and in public. President Nixon considered my questions "valid" and called me "a most spirited reporter," one who asked questions "no man would have the nerve to ask." President Ford told a group of radio and television correspondents that he found it impossible to deter me. And I asked President Carter one of "those questions"—the specific, tough, provocative questions I've become famous for—during his first press conference in the White House.

There have been times when I've had to explain to my fellow reporters just why I ask "those questions." My approach to journalism has been thoroughly misunderstood by editorial writers, by newspaper columnists, and by my colleagues in the White House press corps. But my readers seem to understand that the right answer to one of "those questions" can directly affect people's lives.

"Sarah McClendon may have changed history," said the *New Republic*'s columnist T.R.B. about a question I asked President Eisenhower, and that's just what I was trying to do. When I see something wrong, 1 don't just want to write about it; I want to try to fix it. The right question can do more than produce a news story. It can change government policy—hopefully, for the better.

"My people," as I call my readers, have thanked me again and again for the questions I asked. I keep a special file, which I call Mission Accomplished, filled with letters written by people whose lives were touched by one of my questions. The answer to a question I asked President Nixon about the Veterans Administration affected millions where it counts—in the pocketbook. And my question to President Eisenhower about surplus cabbages resulted in a better diet for starving miners in Kentucky and more money for poor farmers in Texas.

But I've always had my share of critics. United Press International, for instance: "Seldom has a White House press conference question and answer exchange stirred up quite as much intense discussion as . . . when the knuckles of a woman reporter were soundly dusted by President Kennedy," went UPI's story on one of my most controversial questions. "Editors and reporters," the story continued, "not only in Washington but across the country have reacted strongly to the now well identified 'McClendon Incident.' Newspapers, small and large, have carried editorial comment." Unfavorable, I might add. Eric Sevareid once said I had given "rudeness a new dimension."

I never did believe in holding back from a question I thought the public needed to have answered just because someone else had the idea that my asking would be tactless or unmannerly. When I asked seventy-year-old Speaker of the House John W. McCormack about possible retirement plans, he replied, "I'm amazed that you would ask me that. Are there no limits to decency?" Perhaps the worst thing about my questions was my persistence in asking them. Whether I was at a press conference in the White House or behind the scenes, asking questions at the House of Representatives, I kept asking questions until I got an answer. In an editorial statement broadcast over Washington radio station WWDC, the station manager said, "Mrs. McClendon has a way of asking the same question until something gives. We would hate to be in a contest with Sarah McClendon on the other side."

The *Detroit News* called me "the most brazen spotlight

seeker among all of the correspondents haunting the White House," and went on to say that I was "the biggest nuisance ever to question a President." I was the recipient of *Esquire* magazine's Lois Lane Award for my "achievement in rattling Presidents." The *San Francisco Examiner* called me a "plump, reddish-haired news correspondent who has always had a knack of irritating a chief executive." I wonder how they would have described plump, reddish-haired Scotty Reston, columnist for the *New York Times* and the most influential correspondent in Washington.

But no matter how rough it became, I never gave up on what I believed to be my true assignment in Washington: to watch big government from the vantage point of the little taxpayer.

I have done just that since 1944. The unique role that I have played in the Washington press corps was largely a result of my background in small-town journalism combined with the work I've done for the one-woman news service that I have run for over thirty years. Since I am my own boss, I can be more independent than most other reporters. But my feelings about the realities of politics, the feelings that color all my questions, developed long before I arrived up North in Washington, D.C.


I grew up in Tyler, a small town in eastern Texas, a region very different from the rest of Texas. Eastern Texas is geographically and spiritually an extension of the Old South, and has nothing of the rough, masculine ways of the rest of the state. No one from eastern Texas would wear high heeled boots or a cowboy hat except to dress up in costume for a play. Eastern Texans are closer in every way to their neighbors in Louisiana than to other Texans.

My father, Sidney Smith McClendon, arrived in Tyler on a stagecoach from Monroe, Louisiana, his hometown. He opened Tyler's first book and stationery store, where he sold, among other things, musical equipment. This led to my father's interest in music in general and in musical instruments in particular. Father soon became what he called a "piano merchant," and was the Baldwin Company's sole representative in eastern Texas. Since most eastern Texans couldn't afford to buy father's pianos, however, he was forced to create his own credit arrangements with the local farmers. Luckily for Father, his customers were honest.

My mother's family had lived in and around Tyler for generations, and, as lawyers and bankers, thought of themselves as the town aristocrats. Her father (my grandfather) was a judge on the Texas Supreme Court. The family sent sons and daughters to Virginia for schooling. My grandmother moved to Roanoke, Virginia, for three years so that my mother, Annie, and her sisters could attend Hollins College.

Although Mother and Father came from different backgrounds, they had a lot in common. She had studied literature and music at Hollins, and was the founder and guiding light of literary clubs in and around Tyler. They both enjoyed the opera house in our town. He had been very poor as a child, and instead of giving him toys to play with, his mother gave him the Bible and Shakespeare's plays to read. As a youngster, Father memorized long passages of both, and spent many Sunday afternoons in the woods alone, reciting them. Thanks to this early training, my father was one of the finest orators in eastern Texas, and was in great demand to preside over Masonic funerals for over thirty years.

Mother and Father were idealistic, and both were committed to public service. When they were first married, they made a pact to devote a good part of their time to community work. They were great believers in personal participation, and expected the same of each member of their fast-growing family.

I was the youngest of nine children, and it was quite a sight when the entire McClendon family marched into church. As school kids we always marched in town parades. When I was seven, my father dressed me and my sister in little Red Cross uniforms and took us to the post office to sell war bonds. Naturally, when World War I broke out, two of my five brothers were among the first to volunteer to fight. I listened to all the talk about invading oppressors and I believed in what they were doing. I swore that if there was another war when I was older, I'd go too.

Both Mother and Father were active in local politics and interested in national politics, and because of this my whole family, down to the youngest (me), was constantly aware of what public officials in Texas and Washington were up to. We all sat around the porch on summer evenings and talked and argued about politics for hours. In the winter months, we'd move our family debates into the dining room. We often had guests who joined right in, and the times we entertained congressmen were really special. We discussed everything: war and peace, the North and the South, the federal government vs. the states, and local, state, and national candidates for office. Years later, when I read descriptions of John F. Kennedy's childhood, the regular Kennedy family dinner-table debates reminded me of my own childhood.

Father was a loyal Democrat, and for thirty years he

was chairman of the county Democratic committee. He had been deeply involved in Woodrow Wilson's campaign for the presidency in eastern Texas, and when Wilson was elected, my father was named postmaster of Tyler. This meant that my father would be earning a regular salary for the first time. Heretofore, he had been in business for himself. He had been successful, but the income was not lucrative considering that he had a wife and nine children to feed. My father never complained, although living near rich relatives with fewer children, of course, meant that comparisons were often marked. I once heard him say that the amount he had to earn to provide for his family might have been equal to a $100,000 income. But it came and had to go fast just to keep his family fed.

Even though we lived in town, we always had a wonderful garden and plenty of cows for fresh milk. My father could get anything to grow. And we had enough to share our wonderful garden with neighbors, especially widows.

When Father became a postmaster, things were better for us. I never forgot that we had Woodrow Wilson to thank for the food on our table. If he could do for the country what he had done for the McClendons, his place in history was assured.

Although my mother had nine children to raise, she was as interested in local civic affairs and politics as my father, and he was behind her 100 percent. An early advocate of women's rights, Mother attended and spoke at every suffragette meeting that was held in our part of the state. I was too young to go to school in those days, so she would bring me with her. I loved the meetings: The speeches were fiery, the crowds were friendly, and there were usually other children to play with. After a while, I learned most of the speeches by heart, and I loved to stand up on our

dining room table and entertain my family with my version
of suffragette rhetoric. It was a great way for me, the
youngest of nine children, to get everyone to pay attention
to me, and my speeches were such a hit that I ended up on
top of the table every time we had guests. Thanks to my
mother, I started working for women's rights very early
and very young. I guess I've never stopped.

I never considered journalism as a career when I was
growing up in Tyler. I had thought of going in for law,
like numerous other brothers, uncles, and cousins. I knew
I'd have to work for a living—my family, though aristocratic, was hardly rich enough to support me once I was
old enough to get a job.

When I graduated from high school, my sister told me
about an opening on the switchboard at the bank where
she worked. I was hired for the job, and was soon "pro-
moted" to the position of bookkeeper. My job turned out
to be extremely boring, and soon it began to get hateful to
me. The bank became my prison, and I felt as if I was
feeding myself into a machine every day. I knew I'd have
to find another way to earn a living. After listening to me
complain about my job, a local drama teacher who had
come to Tyler from Columbia, Missouri, suggested that I
attend journalism school at the university in her hometown.
School sounded better than the bank, so I saved some
money, borrowed the rest from my brothers and sisters
and family friends, and went to Missouri to become a
newspaper reporter. The journalism school was excellent,
and the training was first-rate and professional, as the
students themselves put out a real daily newspaper filled
with world and local news, not just school news. But the
training was not realistic in one area. The time I spent in
journalism school was about the only period in my news-

paper career when I was not discriminated against simply because I am a woman.

I took to newspaper work immediately. Asking questions came naturally to me and, even more important, as the youngest member of a very large family, I had learned how to *listen,* which every reporter must know how to do. To me, newspaper work meant mobility and independence. After my experience in the bank, this freedom seemed all-important. It still does. But when I graduated from journalism school, I found that east Texas and the rest of the country were in the throes of the Depression. People were out of work everywhere. East Texas had never been the land of opportunity, even in good times, and all roads to a newspaper career seemed to lead to Chicago. But I was painfully shy (which may surprise people who have seen me trying to get recognized at a press conference), and when I arrived in Chicago I was too frightened of the big city to leave my hotel room. I returned to Tyler to worry. My worst nightmare was coming true—I'd never work in journalism.

After two weeks of nonstop terror, I called Carl Estes, the editor of both the *Tyler Courier-Times* and the *Tyler Morning Telegraph,* my hometown papers, to ask for a job. I called at two o'clock on a Sunday afternoon, the very moment when I'd worked up the necessary nerve, and Estes asked me to come in on Monday morning to begin work on a special assignment. My excitement at becoming a reporter at last was mingled with relief at finally finding a job and terror that I'd fail.

When I reported to Estes the next morning, he told me that my job was to get a hospital for Tyler.

I was to be the reporter and investigator of an all-out editorial campaign team employing editorials written by the boss, Carl Estes (husband of the paper's owner, Sarah Butler), and facts collected by me and written in newspaper stories. These stories showed conditions at any local doctors' offices or clinics, the need for hospital beds, the economic worth of a hospital by bringing patients and families to the town from a wide adjacent area, the potentialities of affiliated industries of a hospital center, the attraction for medical talent, the number of serious industrial accidents occurring in connection with a giant oil field—to say nothing of highway accidents occasioned by large amounts of traffic and congestion in communities unprepared to handle huge trucks, trailers with oil pipe, oil and gasoline shipments, and daily travel of workers 50 to 100 miles.

Carl Estes was a crusading, hard-driving editor and publisher with a commanding personality. Few said no to him when he urged acceptance of his ideas. He had driven into our town in a little old Ford, alighted at the newspaper office, and said he would marry the owner. He did. (They later divorced.)

I knew what to do about getting copy for this campaign because I knew the town, the citizens, and the lack of hospital and nursing care. I was on the scene of many of the accidents, and talked to patients as they came in, burned, mangled, or dying.

Besides, I loved crusading for what I thought was for the public good. And I had had a little experience. I had just come from conducting a successful newspaper-editorial campaign in the *Columbian Missourian*, the daily newspaper at the School of Journalism at the University of Missouri, to get passed an ordinance establishing and upgrading the quality of milk sold in the city of Columbia, Missouri. For this I got a top grade in my class on editorial writing under the late famed Dean Roscoe Ellard.

Our town was located just twenty-eight miles from one of the largest oil fields ever discovered, and the world of oil production became superimposed on our small, Old South, Victorian community almost overnight. People from all over the world—technicians, drillers, "con artists," even international gamblers—arrived in Tyler daily. Soon our town was plagued by automobile accidents, drilling accidents, and fires—spillovers from the big eastern Texas oil field eighteen to thirty miles distant. Our hospital facilities —less than twenty beds in a small room on the outskirts of town—were hopelessly inadequate, and Estes and other chamber of commerce types decided we needed something better. We had to get that hospital. And the boss gave me the task.

My job was to find out what it would take to build the hospital, to find out who opposed the project, to find out how to get around that opposition. I saw myself as a fearless, crusading reporter. The pay was ten dollars a week. It didn't take long for disaster to strike, though. In my first week on the job, I uncovered a story some influential citizen did not want written. A complaint was made about me to Estes and wife. I got fired. That was the first of many times that I was caught in a conflict between a special interest, the public interest, and my own hide.

Luckily, like many editors, Carl Estes was a real character, and he rehired me the next day. Estes gave me some excellent early training in the newspaper business. If I could work for Estes, I could work for anyone; so Tom Mahoney of United Press syndicate, New York, told me then. He was right. This was borne out years later when I worked for William Loeb of the *Manchester* (New Hampshire) *Union-Leader*.

By the time Tyler got its new hospital, I was firmly ensconced as one of the two reporters covering our part of east Texas. Floyd Aten, Jr., and I worked well together. He was an ace reporter. But when he wasn't around I wrote most of the stories for that day's paper by myself. Besides working on special projects, like the series of stories I wrote about the hospital, I covered local news and society news for my weekly ten dollars. I never minded working hard, but I hated to be forced to spend my time working on drivel. Editors have been discriminating against women reporters for years by assigning them to write society news. There are legitimate stories to be written for, about, and by women, but the run-of-the-mill society coverage rarely falls into that classification. I'm sure most of the stuff that gets printed about ladies' luncheons is as boring to read as it is to write. Whenever I had to waste my working day on such stories, I always stayed at the *Courier-Times* and worked overtime on the *Morning Telegraph*, too, so that I could get a by-line on a straight news story or two.

There was rarely a dull moment during the eight years I worked for the Tyler newspapers. I recall incurring the anger of County Judge Brady P. Gentry when I refused a carton of cigarettes from him while covering his office. That was my idea of ethics.

There were unexplained deaths by the score. An old couple brutally bludgeoned to death. An all-night look through woods and river bottoms by a photographer, Kenneth Gunn, and myself for a rapist. (I wonder what we would have done if we had found him.) I attended my first stag party—a barbecue for 400 men. I did it because I was beginning my long series of protests against stag parties.

Twice I used aliases in the eastern Texas oil fields— once to visit the homes of two farmers who had just become millionaires from oil produced on their land. They still wore overalls from farming. But they hated reporters and would grant no interviews. Had they known I was a reporter sitting beside their hearth I think these two eccentrics would have harmed me. The other time, I had to assume a new name and vocation to get in to see "Ma" Daugherty and the famed Ironhead Café near Arp, Texas. The café was so called because the proprietor kept an iron chain behind the counter that he could whip out to protect his cash register or remove an unruly customer. Ma said she "never took a dime for a date" in her life. Her girls only danced, she said, and held up their worn-out shoes to prove it. I was doing all right with my disguise until a cousin of mine, Ma's attorney, arrived on legal business and said, "Hello, Sarah."

And never will I forget March 17, 1937. I was coming out of a beauty parlor when someone said a public school had blown up eighteen miles distant in the oil fields and many had been killed. I ran to my office. Gunn, the photographer, and I dashed to his car. In forty-five minutes after 296 people were killed, mostly children, we were on the scene interviewing dazed school officials with bodies lying all over the ground.

I got the last telephone call out of that community for days and informed International News Service, for which I was also a reporter. Then I climbed onto a truck with the wounded to go to the nearest hospital, in Tyler. At last we had our big, adequate hospital, set to open the next day. It opened a day earlier to accommodate the victims of the New London school disaster.

Some good came out of it all. This gas explosion might have been averted had there been an element in the gas to help people detect its odor. From then on, junior chamber of commerce members launched a national drive to put the odorant in gas that today saves many lives.

We often had people complaining about what was written about them in the newspaper. But the saddest thing I ever did was to confront the father of a newborn baby whose birth had been routinely noted by me from hospital reports but who had died before the news hit the parents' friends. It was one of those things that could not have been helped. But the father was hurt.

We had violence at our office, too. An itinerant preacher started preaching nightly in the courthouse square, calling for reforms in our town and attacking some of our leading citizens by name. The victims sought some kind of redress. The preacher also criticized my editor, Carl Estes. Estes reacted with a series of strong editorials, in which, among other things, he invited the preacher to move on.

The preacher, a sturdy man, strode into our newspaper office, demanding to see Estes. Employees sensed a fight. All the men around me hastily exited. The preacher caught Carl. The two of them went down on the floor, both flailing arms, pummeling each other with fists, grappling as they rolled from one side of the room to the other. It clearly looked as if my boss was getting the worst of it. I feared the preacher would kill him by knocking his head against the floor. Tables were overturned. I looked about for something to hit the preacher with and could find only a telephone. I picked it up and came down with it on the preacher's head. That ended the fight.

I worked at the *Courier-Times* for eight years, and during that time I interviewed most of the people who passed through town. Many of them asked why a good reporter like me didn't leave Tyler for a better job on a bigger paper in a bigger town. But I was convinced that no one else would ever hire me. I had a classic eastern Texas insecurity complex that I couldn't shake. Though this complex is really a hangover from Civil War days, it is still strongly felt. People in east Texas seem to have a sense of defeat, of being beaten, before they even try. I had a real fear of the big city, and my experience in Chicago proved to me that I was lucky to be working as a reporter at all. The fact that I am a woman made my dim prospects even dimmer. Even if I ever got a job on another paper, the competition would surely prove too much for me and I would be fired, I felt. I think I would have worked for the *Tyler Courier-Times* for the rest of my life if they hadn't finally fired me for good.

Carl Estes, my first editor, who had often received complaints about my uncovering stories some people in our town did not want to be written, had moved on to another paper, and my new editor asked me to help the chamber of commerce block the construction of an iron ore plant scheduled to be built in Rusk, Texas, forty-six miles distant, which many felt would have helped the region's economy. I knew the area needed that plant—my father had told me so for years. I couldn't understand (and I never did) why the chamber of commerce was opposed to the plant, since attracting local industry was their main function. But my editor had promised the local businessmen that no more stories about the plant would appear in either the *Courier-Times* or the *Morning Telegraph*. I didn't realize how serious that prohibition was, wrote the story my way, embarrassed my editor, and was fired. I later learned several groups—bankers, clandestine or "hot oil" producers—took the credit for my departure. It is hard to know exactly who was responsible. But getting fired was the best thing that could have happened to me. I wanted to keep working as a reporter, so, to avoid the agony of job hunting, I started a one-woman news service in Tyler. I became the regional correspondent for papers in Houston, Dallas, Fort Worth, and Shreveport. I even wrote about goings-on in eastern Texas for a New York City trade paper devoted to the shoe business. After a year and a half of running my news service, I was offered a job as a reporter by the editor of the *Beaumont Enterprise*.

I applied for the job and much to my surprise was accepted. I had been recommended for the job by a colleague who thought I was wasting my talent for reporting in a small town that was cut off from the rest of Texas as well as from the rest of the world. Accepting the job would mean leaving Tyler. It would mean joining the Newspaper Guild, a long way from being a hometown reporter. It would also mean, at age twenty-eight, growing up. If I moved to Beaumont, I would be on my own for the first time, away from my parents and my brothers and sisters. Would I be good enough to work on the *Enterprise*? Brave enough to live alone? I thought it through and decided to accept the offer. I wanted to make it as a newspaper reporter in the real world, not just in my hometown. I never lived in Tyler again.

In Beaumont I covered everything from the federal courts to the waterfront—literally. I loved my job, and I loved the independent feeling I had living away from Tyler. But my career on the *Enterprise* was cut short by the outbreak of World War II. When war was declared, I decided to make good on my childhood pledge to join the army. I believed myself too good to join the Women's Army Auxiliary Corps. My lifelong interest in the military first developed when I was working for the *Enterprise*. But when my editor assigned me to cover the local WACs instead of General Eisenhower, who was on maneuvers with his troops a few miles out of Beaumont, I couldn't resist making fun of the Women's Army Corps in my stories and in my private conversations. Next to Ike and his men, the WACs looked silly and ineffectual. Stupid, asinine women I called them, and I applied to join military intelligence. When I was told only lawyers and people in uniform were accepted into the program, I enlisted. When I appeared in Houston to take the oath, a colonel who had read some of my perfectly wicked stories looked at me in amazement and said, "What, you?"

My family was horrified. They were all for marching in parades and selling war bonds, but joining the WACs was going too far. They accepted the fact that I'd converted to Catholicism, and bore with me when I threatened to become a nun, but no "lady" joined the army. My boyfriend, who was in the army himself, wanted me on a pedestal, not in a uniform, and broke up with me in disgust. It wasn't the first or the last time I lost a man by being too independent.

The day before I left Texas for basic training, I auctioned off all my civilian clothes except one blue suit and a pair of high heeled shoes, and paid off my charge accounts at local stores. But when I arrived at WAC headquarters, no uniforms were available. I spent my first two weeks in the army drilling in the mud in my suit and high heels, the only clothes I owned. Some months later, after basic training and officer candidate school, I applied again to join military intelligence. This time, some former Texas newspaper colleagues, now in the army, had recommended me to take over public relations running of the WAC Training Center at Fort Oglethorpe, Georgia. A good soldier, I obeyed my orders and gave up the dream of military intelligence. I concentrated on learning my new job. I found public relations fascinating, and I got so good at what I was doing that

I was transferred to work at the Pentagon in Washington. The orders named me specifically—something unusual in the army.

Naturally, my new orders scared me to death. Washington was not only the big city, it was the North. In eastern Texas we all knew that people from the North and the East were much smarter than we were, much better in every way. I didn't know if I'd ever find my way around the Pentagon—what a building to be lost in!

I moved to Washington, and though I loved my work, I soon felt alone and unhappy. As liaison between WAC headquarters and the Army Bureau of Public Relations, I met a lot of people. My job was to answer questions and supply ideas for newspaper and magazine articles about WACs for the rest of the army and the rest of the world. I met countless newspaper reporters, photographers, filmmakers, and representatives of every form of media and communication. But people were not *nice* to women in uniform. The men who were in the army didn't want us, and neither did the civilians. I was so lonely that I leaped at the chance to marry a man who was obviously on the rebound from and still in love with another woman. The marriage didn't work at all—he went back to his girlfriend within a few months—and I found myself alone again, but with one big difference: I was pregnant. I managed (and managed and managed) to work for eight months, and then I told my boss that I had to quit. I was still wearing my regulation WAC uniform, and he hadn't noticed!

I worked at home for a month as a speechwriter, thanks to the contacts I had made doing public relations for the army. When it was time for the baby to be born, I took a taxi to Walter Reed Hospital. Since I was a first lieutenant,

I insisted on my full rights and privileges as an officer, which upset the people at Walter Reed no end. They tried to talk me out of it, but I became the first army officer to give birth at a military hospital.

When I returned home with my new daughter, Sally, there was no question in my mind that the two of us would stay in Washington. By then, I had been away from home too long to move back to Texas. I was sure my family would tell me how to raise my child and how to live if I did go back. I had learned as much as I needed to know about working on Texas newspapers, so there was no future for me back home either personally or professionally. I decided to try to use my newspaper experience and my public relations contacts to find a job in Washington. I wrote letters to several editors offering my services as a reporter.

When Sally was nine days old, I left her at home with a baby-sitter while I went downtown for a doctor's appointment. Taking advantage of my first moment of freedom since I entered Walter Reed, I stopped off at the National Press Building on my way home to see Bascom Timmons, the Washington correspondent for a number of newspapers in Texas and elsewhere and one of the men to whom I'd sent a letter. Many of the men who normally staffed Timmons's bureau were away in the military services, and when he realized that I was an experienced newspaper reporter, he wouldn't let me out of the office. I sat down to work then and there, first calling my baby-sitter to request her to stay with Sally until I could get home that evening. I never told Timmons that I had a tiny daughter. He was the kind of man who picked up stray kittens on the streets, and I knew he would want me to stay at home. But I knew I had to work to support my child.

Timmons's office manager (a man, naturally) was furious that a woman had been hired to work in his office. Like many newspapermen, he didn't like women. "You'll only be here a few days," he told me the day I started work. I stayed for two and a half years. As I left work on Christmas Eve to go home to Sally both years, this same office manager told me my job would not be waiting when I got back. With more than ten years' experience as a reporter in Texas behind me, I was not too surprised by his attitude, although I was greatly worried. This antiwoman bias has followed me since I left journalism school.

"McClendon, you're supposed to get a raise," they told me in Tyler, "but Joe's wife is going to have a baby, so he'll get the raise instead of you. After all, he has a family to feed." Or, "McClendon, you're supposed to get a raise, but Ben has to drive a long way to work every day. He's got to have a raise so he can get a new car."

When I first started working at the *Courier-Times*, I smoked cigarettes. After I'd been there a day or two, Carl Estes put up a sign that read: "No lady on this staff will be seen smoking in public." Actually, Estes did me a favor when he put up that sign, because I stopped smoking then and never smoked again.

Timmons assigned me to be the Washington correspondent for the *Philadelphia Daily News*, an account he had been too busy to write for. I was given a private office and a White House press pass. Timmons suggested that I go to Capitol Hill to get my stories, but for my first month on the job, I was too weak to open the big doors at the House of Representatives. I would climb the steps, a job in itself, and wait at a door for someone else to come in or go out. Once inside the door, I walked from office to office, trying to get a story from the congressmen from

Pennsylvania. At first, I didn't know anything about their problems and they didn't know me, but we both learned, and several people I met then are still news sources for me today.

When the men who used to work for Timmons's bureau started returning home from the war, Timmons told me he'd have to give them their jobs back. That meant I'd have to go. "You should be like May Craig," Timmons told me (May, a veteran Washington newswoman, was one of my professional heroines), "you should have your own news bureau," and he proceeded to help me start one. He gave me accounts which he was too busy to handle himself. On the strength of these and the few clients Timmons had allowed me to acquire on my own (the *Beaumont Enterprise* was one), I went into business for myself as a Washington correspondent.

I've never gotten rich, I've never made a lot of money, but I earned enough to keep myself going, to support my daughter, and to be independent. No one tells me what to write. I see reporters who work for the big bureaus, for the *New York Times*, for instance, or the *Philadelphia Inquirer*, who report on one subject all the time, like the Department of Health, Education and Welfare or the patent office. I have always been thankful that I didn't have to stick to writing one kind of story, covering one kind of beat.

Instead, I covered Capitol Hill, the State Department, the Veterans Administration, the FBI, and the White House, or any place else where I thought there was a story. I could develop my own stories, go where I wanted to go, see the people I wanted to see. Running my own news bureau was a great opportunity, and I was determined to make the most of it.

# 2

## Scared of FDR, Relaxed with Harry

Franklin D. Roosevelt was in the White House when I became a Washington correspondent in 1944. I went there frequently and checked out many a query, but I always felt I could get more news and get it more forthrightly at the Capitol. I did go to his press conferences and also covered Mrs. Roosevelt's press conferences, which were for women only. I spent most of my time at the House of Representatives, my first love, where I still feel government policy is being made on the most personal and understandable level. I believed then, as I believe now, that my stories from Washington should help my readers in Texas, New Hampshire, Wisconsin, or Philadelphia understand what the government was doing and how it affected them personally. The House was the place to find out.

The Roosevelt press conferences that I observed (as I've said, I was much too frightened and too shy to participate and too ignorant to ask a question—I was terrified that my questions would reveal how much I didn't know) were stilted, privileged affairs. Although he held frequent press conferences, Roosevelt favored well-known reporters who were well established in their careers. The way these reporters questioned FDR was very different from the way reporters ask a president questions today. "Would the president entertain a question on taxes?" I remember one reporter asking Roosevelt. It seemed more like a tea party than a press conference, more like the House of Lords than the White House.

While a few of FDR's favorite reporters were seated in the chairs on either side of the president (May Craig and broadcaster Earl Godwin were two of the fortunate few), the rest of us fought for standing room in the overcrowded Oval Office. It's not easy to write standing up, and we used to brace our notebooks on each other's back, crowded in like sardines. I'm quite sure now that Roosevelt's press secretary, Steve Early, must have filled in reporters later with what they missed, for it was impossible to take adequate notes. The acoustics were poor also, and it is remarkable indeed that so many important stories came out of these meetings.

To make things worse, many of the reporters were so afraid of Roosevelt's biting sarcasm that they did not ask questions at all. Don't forget, reporters were *scared* in those days. They were afraid that their bosses would criticize them and that their publishers would be embarrassed. And they were right—editors and publishers are for the most part very conservative people. I've been turned down as a correspondent by many an editor because I've become well known as a reporter who asked provocative questions that were not always easy to answer.

President Truman really did the press a favor when he took us out of the Oval Office and across the street to the old Indian Treaty Room on the fourth floor of the building which once housed the departments of war, navy, and state. What a difference the new room made! Reporters could actually sit down as they took notes.

But this change didn't really affect me. I still spent more

time on Capitol Hill than I did at the White House, covering the congressmen who represented my readers. I found the House and the Senate fascinating. There was always so much going on that there was never a lack of material for the stories I hoped would make the workings of the government more meaningful for my people. Congress was more specific than the White House when it came to dealing with specific issues. They were closer to reality. The White House has been known to be concerned with "larger issues." I left those issues to the wire services to write about.

As I grew more knowledgeable about the ways of Washington, however, I learned that to become a truly effective reporter, I would have to cover both Congress and the White House. I learned that if a visitor from Texas went to see the president in the morning, and if the White House press staff wouldn't give out any information on the meeting, I could catch that Texan in the afternoon up on the hill in his senator's or congressman's office. Then I would corner the visitor and find out for myself what happened. I started spending more time at the White House.

Shuttling between Capitol Hill and the White House added depth to my Washington coverage. For example, I was very much aware of President Truman's unpopularity in east Texas. The people from my part of the country hated Truman so much that their hatred spread to the government itself and to the city where the laws were made. In Tyler, people thought of Washington, D.C., as the embodiment of evil. While Truman was president, one of my brothers asked me how I could live in "that horrible city." Why should I have anything to do with "lying, crooked, sneaky big government?" My brother and most of his neighbors felt they were being held down and held back by unnecessary government regulations. Farmers who grew black-eyed peas, for instance, were being forced to grow their crop according to regulations put out by the Office of Price Administration, which, like as not, were written by a man from California seated behind a desk in Washington who had never tasted black-eyed peas and did not know how sturdy and nutritious they were. My father always said he never passed a field of them without tipping his hat because they kept so many people in the South from starving to death after the Civil War.

People in Texas also deeply resented Truman's price controls on oil and other commodities. They saw in these controls a sign of ever increasing government domination over their lives. At the House of Representatives I found out that other parts of the country felt the same way. Delegations of enraged constituents would arrive daily at congressional offices, armed with signed petitions complaining about Truman, partisanship, cronyism, and scandal.

The Truman administration also was besmirched by Democrats who apparently did not care as much about sullying the name of their chief source of power, their leader, as they wanted to make money. Electric refrigerators (then a luxury), mink coats, and 5 percent commissions for influence peddling in government were a way of life during this period.

Major General Harry H. Vaughan, Truman's old buddy from World War I and his military aide in the White House, let a donor send an electric refrigerator to Mrs. Truman at the White House, and to others in the Truman administration. Mrs. Truman apparently did not understand what it was or what was going on when the gift arrived, so she told attendants to take it over to the White House mess. This was where the administrative aides ate. There it served a number of employees.

(The refrigerators were, ironically, made of wood on

the outside; they were manufacturers' experimental models. At least one mink coat was obtained by one of Truman's secretaries, but it is reported to have come to her as a gift from her husband, who accepted a loan to buy it from a man who wanted to be close to the Truman hierarchy. The lender was from a Washington law firm whose principals liked to drop names about the influential officials they knew in government.)

A 5 percenter was a lobbyist, consultant, or commission man who took for his fee that much of a return from the total contract, settlement, or profit he had managed to procure from the government for his client. Nowadays in Washington, 5 percenters call themselves consultants and charge more.

Besides being unpopular with a large portion of the electorate, Truman was constantly doing battle with Congress. He turned this conflict into a campaign issue when he ran in 1948. (Gerald Ford did the same thing in 1976, unsuccessfully.)

I never really got to know Truman very well, which I now regret. I was younger then, and inexperienced in the ways of presidents. There were too many stars in my eyes in those days for me to get a good hard look at Harry Truman. But now, the more I learn (or remember) about Truman, the more I respect him for his courage and his character. He was called on to fill a huge gap, and he had to do it immediately, with very little knowledge of what had been going on at the White House. Luckily, he was a fast learner.

Truman turned out to be a surprise to a lot of people, me included. When he first entered office, Truman was looked down on and made fun of because he was not an "intellectual." (The same happened to Lyndon B. Johnson.)

Career State Department men would brief Truman as if he knew nothing at all. He got tired of people assuming he was ignorant, but he didn't make a fuss about it. Truman was probably the most humble president in history. He knew that all the fuss, all the trappings, were for the office, not the man. After being sworn in as president, many men become haughty and think that they have been divinely sent to fill the job. I believe that Harry S. Truman was one president who never lost touch with the people back home.

This was made clear to me years later when I was going through the Harry S. Truman Library at Independence, Missouri, with Sue Gentry, who has made a career of Truman history. Gentry told me that whenever Truman ran into a group of visitors going through the library, he would stage an impromptu press conference, taking questions on all subjects, explaining his answers to youngsters and to their parents. Harry Truman was never a snob, and was never afraid to tell the truth to anybody.

Having grown up in eastern Texas, I was used to the courteous manners and at times flattering attitudes of the Old South. When I went to college in Missouri, I found the people there to be shockingly frank, often crude, but always truthful. That was Truman. He was a man of positive ideas, and had a warm, down-to-earth personality. He could cut through the veneer and red tape of government with a few simple words. His approach to a subject was never circular.

Truman's directness of speech transformed the press conferences I attended into more informal affairs, with a lot of give-and-take between the president and the reporters. Truman's answers were always short and blunt. I always picture him barking back an answer to a reporter. One morning, reporters were slow in asking questions.

After a few hesitations, Truman said, "Well, I guess that's all, boys," and ended it in six minutes.

In the course of my trips to Truman's White House, I had become friendly with one of the White House guards. He claimed to be a great fisherman on his days off, and when he heard that I had never eaten a Chincoteague oyster, a local specialty, he was aghast and promised to give me some from his next catch. One day I got a phone call to come to the White House and pick up my oysters.

Well, I thought, this must be the most peculiar reason why a reporter ever went to the White House. I picked up my oysters on a Saturday morning, put them aside, and decided, as long as I was there anyway, to check out the White House for news. Immediately, in the foyer, I ran into Vice-President Alben Barkley of Kentucky, a delightful man who seemed to know everyone. He and I were having a nice chat when he heard someone calling "Barkley! Barkley!" With that, Truman craned his neck around a column in the rear of the lobby.

"Barkley, where are you?" he asked. "Oh," he continued, "I might have known you would be talking to a pretty woman." The vice-president had to rush off. As I watched him go, I thought, it is not every person who can be talking to the vice-president and have the president of the United States interrupt the conversation.

Truman was a very likable man. He said he drank bourbon and he did. He said that he played poker and he did (usually with newspapermen). You have to like somebody like that.

After he left the presidency, Truman returned to Washington for the funeral of a man he admired greatly, General George C. Marshall. After the ceremony, I went to Truman's suite at the Mayflower Hotel to see what news I could pick up. I found him pouring himself four fingers of whiskey unabashedly before me and looking forward to a drink with old friends from other days. How few presidents (or ex-presidents), I remember thinking, would be honest enough to do that before a newspaper reporter.

# 3

# *Ike Blows His Fuse*

By the time Dwight D. Eisenhower was elected president, I was giving more attention to national issues. I had watched the political maneuverings at the national convention that produced Eisenhower for the presidency. I had also been observing the other female members of the Washington press corps long enough to realize that some of them were more successful and better known than others. They had images, and they had them because they went out and created them. Nothing happens by chance: There must be a cause before there is an effect. Esther van Wagoner Tufty, a reporter with an aristocratic manner who convinced most of Washington to call her "the Duchess," was a prime example of such a success story. I had been sitting on my hands, being a quiet reporter. Now I felt I could be better at my job if I changed my style. If I wanted to get a story, I'd have to *participate*. I decided to try to make myself heard.

I went to Eisenhower's first press conference, anxious to see how he would treat the press. I had seen him evade the press as chief of staff, and I was determined he would not get by with that now. But I found some obstacles in my way.

The American people looked forward to this change in administrations and Ike was popular. So many reporters had arrived for the conference that the old Indian Treaty Room on the fourth floor of the Executive Office Building had filled quickly and there were no seats left. I had to climb the stairs to the balcony. Oh, what a pity, I thought. My colleagues had indicated that no one would ask a question from up there, and if they did, they would not be recognized. And there were no seats in the balcony so I had to stand.

The second obstacle to my plan was Eisenhower himself. He hated press conferences, but he thought he ought to hold them. He knew their importance from his days as commander of Allied Forces in Europe, where he had a topnotch professional to head public relations in Major General A. D. Surles. So, like a good soldier, he scheduled regular meetings with the press, weekly if possible, and even improved on the format. He should be given credit for this. It was Eisenhower who created the press conference as we know it today when he allowed these sessions to be taped, edited (to improve on Ike's often poor language), and shown on the air. (In other landmark moments of press conference history, Kennedy introduced live broadcasts, Nixon filled in the White House swimming pool on the west side to give us the wonderful press center in which we work today on two floors with assembly rooms, and Ford and Carter began to call on reporters sitting in the back of the room, on blacks, and on women besides Helen Thomas of United Press International and me. Ford also let reporters for the first time have a follow-up question. This cut down the number of questions that could be asked on different subjects and likewise the number of reporters who could get in with a question. Carter has control over press conferences in his own way. He does not let reporters attract him—he picks them out. But it was Eisenhower who first made televised press conferences a hit with the public.)

Although Eisenhower agreed to hold press conferences, he never planned to expose himself to criticism by reporters, especially not while millions would be watching at home on television.

At his first press conference, I watched him from the balcony as he walked out in front of the crowd, read us a long statement, and seemed about to leave. I couldn't believe it! Didn't he plan to take questions? I expected the crowd to explode with questions, but the rest of the reporters were silent. It was now or never.

"Mr. President," I called down from the balcony, "is this going to be the format of your future press conferences, or will reporters be able to ask questions on matters of public interest?"

Eisenhower looked up at me as if he were in pain. But he did answer my question, saying yes, he would be taking questions at future press conferences. The other reporters were more horrified than Ike. Not only had I dared to challenge the president, I did it from the balcony! Clearly, I was not a polite reporter. But I had a question and I felt I should ask it, no matter where I was. After all, others were letting him get by with what I feared might become precedent. From then on, though, I arrived at press conferences early and made sure I sat in one of the first few rows.

From my front seat, I kept forcing myself to get up and ask questions. A presidential press conference was a wonderful opportunity to get a story, and I wanted to make the most of it. Much to my surprise, after I started speaking up at Ike's press conferences, I started receiving invitations to other press conferences.

"You stir things up," one of Ike's cabinet members told me.

Later, I was to get encouragement from one of the members of President Nixon's cabinet. When he was Secretary of Defense, Melvin R. Laird presented me with a gadget at a party in my honor. It had a whistle on one end and a flashlight on the other. "Use this, Sarah, to get attention at presidential press conferences," he said.

Government officials saw in me the chance to get away from dull, routine, technical questions, because, they often told me, my questions were specific and were often asked from a different wavelength than most reporters used. By asking a question that would be meaningful to readers in Texas, New England, or South Carolina, I added interest and excitement to the sessions. This, I am sure, happened because many regional problems in America today spill over into other regions, and since I asked questions about cities and people away from the Washington–New York corridor, they produced welcome variety.

I always tried to pick out questions that were on the minds of the people. If I discovered a trend in a problem affecting several scattered states, then I knew I would be on the right track in tapping an issue of wide interest to people. It might not be of any interest to the Washington correspondents who were dealing mostly with problems developing in the capital. But, then, I was not aiming at them.

There was another angle to it. I was cautioned by my first editors in Washington not to duplicate the wire services that would be dealing with the obvious top national issues. I sometimes chose a sideline or a continuation of a national event. But the record will show that I did not confine my questions to local or parochial issues, as some Washington correspondents became fond of characterizing me. I'll put my record for raising questions of widespread interest against anyone else who ever covered Washington.

If I asked a question about a tin smelter on the Texas Gulf Coast, which helped set the world price on scarce tin, I had to identify with my nearest paper, the *Port Arthur News*. If I asked about illegal aliens troubling El Paso people 900 miles distant, I identified with the *El Paso Times*.

My questions were appreciated by the public, judging from the response I got from my readers and the people who saw me on television. People from all over the country sent me letters and called me on the phone with suggestions for questions they wanted answered. I could rarely use these questions, however, as they usually reflected interests that were too self-serving.

Besides, I think of my own questions. There are obvious questions that will be asked at any press conference, but the wire services generally ask those. I thought it was my job to ask something special, or unusual, or different— being a regional reporter, I had to. Writing for people in Texas, Pennsylvania, and the other regions where my clients published newspapers led me to ask about subjects the other reporters didn't know or care about. The other reporters did not understand my questions, which led to their lack of understanding of *me*.

Ike didn't understand why I wrote for so many different newspapers, which led him to turn the tables on me and ask me a question at one of his press conferences. In those days, by the official rules of the presidential press conference, a reporter stood up and gave his name and the name of the paper he worked for before he asked his question. We don't do that today, because the White

House has changed the rules, probably because it gave individual reporters too much publicity and too much notoriety, so some White House reporters alleged.

I wrote for many different papers, and I used to name a different paper almost every time I asked Ike a question. Questions on oil were dear to the heart of my readers in Texas, but when I asked a question about the shoe industry or the overhaul of the Portsmouth Naval Shipyard, I was working for my readers in Manchester, New Hampshire. Once when I posed a question to Ike, he said, "Let me ask you a question first. Do you get fired every week and go to work for another paper the next week?"

Naturally, everyone howled at Ike's joke. (I always thought someone on his staff had put him up to this.) "I try to represent all my clients," I told him, and Ike said he thought "that was fair." But the laughter continued and, in some ways, it has followed me for the rest of my career.

They laughed when I asked Ike if there wasn't some way for the United States government to transport 400 acres' worth of green cabbages that were being plowed under in southern Texas to Harlan County, Kentucky, where people were living on government surplus food, mostly starches. Most of those people hadn't had any green in their diets for six months.

Ike responded beautifully. "I'll look into it and find out if it's possible. I like cabbage very much myself."

I stayed on the cabbage story, and it became a story of how government really works. A few days after I asked Ike about the cabbages, the secretary of agriculture held a press conference about the cabbages, and so did Jim Hagerty, Eisenhower's press secretary. The senator from Kentucky, John Sherman Cooper, asked his staff to work on the problem over the Labor Day weekend, which they did. The Department of Agriculture made studies of the problem, as did the Interstate Commerce Commission, the American Association of Railroads, and the Department of Commerce. But not one bureaucrat could come up with a way to get around the shipping conference rules as to what you can charge for commodities sent from one state to another and how you can send them when not shipped privately and noncommercially. We found we could not placate all the commissions concerned, so volunteers from the Salvation Army ended up taking the cabbages from Texas to Kentucky by truck. I put the cabbage story in my Mission Accomplished file.

The other reporters thought my question had been so silly, so stupid. They laughed and giggled about it, and cute little stories started popping up in their newspapers about that cabbage story. No one focused on the sluggishness of the government which came to light or on the human beings involved, not only the ones who were starving in Kentucky, but the farmers in Texas who couldn't sell their crops. How would they feed their families, keep their children's schools open? I'm still proud that I asked that "funny" question about cabbages.

When I asked Eisenhower a question about dam construction, a subject that was under discussion in Congress at that time (and a subject people are finally starting to be interested in, thanks to their raised ecological consciousness), the boys—the special White House correspondents—had never heard anything about it, and made fun of me and my question again. But I knew that there was a controversy between the army engineers who wanted to build huge dams downstream and the group who opposed them, such as Representative W. R. Poage of Texas, who said it was smarter to collect the water and conserve it up-stream, where it fell. These upstream dams could be smaller, cheaper, and could provide more effective protection against floods. I asked Ike if he favored large downstream or small upstream dams. He replied that he didn't know, and that was true.

"What is this silly woman talking about?" my fellow journalists asked, and some of them continue to ask that to this day.

Some months after I asked my dam question, Eisenhower told us during a press conference that he had just finished reading a book called *Big Dam Foolishness*. "If you boys remember," he said, "a very valid, good question came up about dams just a while ago."

Good for Eisenhower! The poor man was learning. We reporters really had to educate him because he knew so little about government. I give him great credit, though. Although he didn't want to meet with the press, he faced up to his duty and did it. And part of his duty was answering Sarah McClendon's questions, even though it some-times infuriated him. His fuse was short, and some of my questions made him visibly angry. His wife, Mamie, I heard, dedicated her life to trying to keep him calm, trying to keep the vein in his temple from beginning to throb. But I wasn't married to him, and I had a job to do and questions to ask. Some of my colleagues accused me of deliberately wanting to "torment" the president, and some said I was trying to give him a heart attack.

There was a picture on exhibit at the National Press Club of Ike getting mad because of a question I'd asked. I don't remember which question it was (it happened so many times), but in this picture he is the maddest human being I have ever seen. There's no caption to the picture, but all the members know it's Sarah McClendon who made Ike look like that.

People were even afraid I'd upset Mamie. I had been invited to a big party with a top-drawer guest list. Parties are one of a reporter's best sources for stories. I try to talk to as many people as I can at a party, and I always get a lot of leads. I love parties as social events, too, and I was terribly excited about attending this one.

When Mamie Eisenhower accepted her invitation to the same party, mine was canceled. My hostess thought that Mamie wouldn't appreciate seeing me there because of the effect I had on her husband's blood pressure. Thank goodness Ike and his press staff were not that sensitive.

"Sarah, we'll always take your questions," Jim Hagerty once told me, and he went on to tell me why. At one of Ike's cabinet meetings, several members of Ike's cabinet, former big-business men with very little experience in government, urged the president not to call on me anymore. I wrote for small, unimportant papers that they didn't read and that no one they knew read. I was just an unimportant woman from the wrong part of the country. But then, according to Hagerty, a staff official, the late I. Jack Martin, spoke up for me. "Mr. President," he said, "I know this girl. She used to come to my office when I worked for Senator Bob Taft on Capitol Hill. She knows what's going on at the grass roots, and she will always ask you a question that reflects the people's thinking. Mr. President, you need to know what people are thinking." Eisenhower agreed to continue to recognize me.

Not that it would have been easy to ignore me. I'd learned a lot since I sang my first question down at Eisenhower from the balcony. Press conferences are all alike: First the wire services are heard (AP will go first one time,

UPI the next), then the networks, then some of the larger bureaus, and then we just fight for the right to be recognized. I jumped up quicker, spoke louder, and was more determined than other reporters, so I was recognized regularly. Sometimes my aggressiveness embarrassed my editors, the most conservative of men. To this day, my editors cringe when they hear a remark about "that Sarah." I've gotten used to it by now—why can't they?

Two of my editors (Frank W. Mayborn from Temple, Texas, and Harry Provence from Waco, Texas) were sitting with me at a press conference when I asked Eisenhower why he spent so much time away from the White House and its responsibilities, playing golf, instead of pushing for a proposed public works project which one of my newspapers supported. In his answer, Ike stuck to the merits of the project and didn't mention his golf game. My editors thought that question was totally out of line. They didn't think I had the *right* to ask the president a question like that. When will people realize that the president works for *us*, that we pay his salary? He must answer to the voters, and it was my job to ask the questions.

Later, I realized that Ike's golf games were part of a health and exercise plan prescribed by his doctors. I sent him an apology, and he sent me a charming note in return, accepting my apology. I framed his letter and I still have it today. "No apology was needed," Ike wrote, "because I am sure that you had a special interest in the matter of community public works."

It was my most controversial editor, William Loeb of the *Manchester Union-Leader*, who first suggested that I ask Jim Hagerty whether Sherman Adams had received a gift of a vicuña coat from New England industrialist Bernard Goldfine. At that time, Adams was the top assistant to the president and the second most powerful man in the United States. Although I could hardly believe Loeb's tip (Adams was "on the take," Loeb said, and had been receiving personal gifts, including a vicuña coat and a rug, from a New England textile manufacturer), I asked Hagerty about it at a White House press briefing. The other reporters hooted and moaned and groaned when I asked about Adams and, for once, I must say I couldn't blame them. I knew Adams. He was a former governor of New Hampshire, and I'd covered him many times for the *Union-Leader* while he was an official at the State Department. He was respected by everyone. Why would a man with so much to lose risk it all for a few gifts? Hagerty didn't believe the tip either. He pooh-poohed the idea as ridiculous and passed it off as impossible. But when I asked him to check it out, he said he would and I believed him.

Hagerty was the best presidential press secretary I ever worked with. He told us the news calmly, quietly, and honestly. Reporters didn't argue with Jim Hagerty. We trusted him. Always businesslike, Hagerty returned my phone calls and answered my questions.

To both Hagerty's and my surprise, the story turned out to be true. Eisenhower, faced with scandal and with the loss of his closest and most valuable aide, reacted like a soldier: He ordered Adams to testify before Congress immediately. I met Adams and his wife at the door of the House Office Building as they were going into one of the hearings. I felt desperately sorry for her, but when he stared at me with his steely, cold eyes, I looked right back at him. I had nothing to be ashamed of: Exposing Adams had been a public service.

As the story of the gifts unfolded, the president realized Adams would have to go. Sherman Adams resigned and retired to a life of virtual isolation in New Hampshire. It was a terrible comedown from the ivory tower of the White House, especially for a man who had worked so hard on Eisenhower's campaign in the first place. Sherman Adams thought he was so important to Eisenhower's election effort that once, during a campaign trip, he had Mrs. Eisenhower moved out of Ike's hotel suite so that he could move in and be closer to the candidate. At the next stop, Mamie saw to it that her things were put in Ike's room while Adams was given a room on another floor.

It was my independence and my weakness for the underdog that first led me to start working for William Loeb, the man who gave me the Sherman Adams scoop. A friend of mine could not accept the job as Loeb's Washington correspondent and recommended me to Loeb as her successor. Since I was in business for myself, I always welcomed new clients, and the fact that most people seemed to talk about Loeb with a combination of hatred and fear just kindled my interest. Besides, I was ready to branch out and learn about another part of the country. Les and Liz Carpenter were also trying to get to represent Loeb's papers at this time. They lost out and I won.

Meeting and working with the people of New Hampshire turned out to be the best part of my experience with Loeb. Most of the people I met were very naive about issues that directly concerned them, and had no idea how to get money out of the federal government for projects in their state. By contrast, Texans were professionals at that. Necessity and a powerful, flamboyant United States senator, Tom Connally, taught them how. Texas was hit especially hard by the Depression, and when money was needed for hurricane or flood relief, or to build dams, the money had to come from the federal government, since there were no local funds to draw on. Senator Connally worked tirelessly in Washington to see that Texans got the funds they needed. He visited the White House almost every day, and personally appeared at each agency that might part with some federal dollars.

Loeb was always nice to me and, aside from an occasional tip, left me alone when it came to news stories. In fact, he would visit Washington without ever coming to see me, his Washington correspondent. Whenever I would bump into him on Capitol Hill, I assumed he was there to check up on me. But Loeb didn't call me in Washington because he was there on his own private business that had nothing to do with me and my stories. Loeb visited senators and congressmen regularly. He was not as naive as his readers were when it came to getting help from the government.

Loeb did control the rest of the stories in the *Union-Leader*, and he has been known to use his newspaper like a club against someone he doesn't like. He pilloried Ed Muskie when the senator was running for President just because he didn't share his political views. I think a newspaper should be run for the good of the general public, but Loeb makes the mistake of presenting his own special interests, biases, and enmities as news. He finally fired me when I informed him about the duplicity of a candidate endorsed by the *Union-Leader*. I had been sending Loeb damaging memos about his candidate, which showed him to be a dishonest man who specialized in influence peddling. I guess I was telling Loeb more than he wanted to know. Years later he hired me back again. I needed the money. The job turned out to be temporary. I wouldn't work for him anymore.

Although Ike seemed to stay very calm during the Sherman Adams scandal, he exploded when I asked him at one of his press conferences if he was planning to use United States troops in Lebanon without first consulting Congress as the Constitution required him to. My question really hit a nerve. Eisenhower used to make frequent appearances on Capitol Hill when he was a general in the army to testify on military issues, and he thought he had the respect of Congress. He certainly knew more about the army (and the marines) than they did, and everybody knew it. It was difficult for him to go to them to ask for advice. It is easy for a president to get carried away with his own power, especially in what he believes to be an emergency. Time is short—why waste it consulting with people who don't really understand? When a problem occurs, the Department of Defense and the State Department hand the president what they have decided is the right policy and the president acts. Sometimes the president informs members of Congress of what he is planning to do, but in an emergency he will rarely consult with them first. After all, what if they disagree?

When I asked Eisenhower my question about the marines in Lebanon, I forced the executive branch to recognize its constitutional priorities. Possibly, I kept Ike from committing even more troops. T.R.B., the *New Republic*'s Washington correspondent, agreed and wrote in his column, "Sarah McClendon may have changed history."

I tugged at history again at a press conference in the final year of Ike's term. Richard Nixon, Ike's vice-president, had begun his campaign against John F. Kennedy for the presidency. Eisenhower was trying to build Nixon up, to tell us what a good vice-president he had been. It was so obviously "make talk" that all the reporters wondered who could have put Ike up to it. I was tired of the propaganda and wanted some specific information that I could use in a story. I got up and asked, "Mr. President, could you tell us what policy decisions Vice-President Nixon has helped make?"

No, he said, he couldn't think of any.

Later during the same press conference, Charles Mohr, another reporter, gave Eisenhower the chance to salvage Nixon's reputation as a valuable member of his administration. "Mr. President," Mohr asked, "can't you think of anything that Nixon did?"

"Give me a week and I'll think of something" was Ike's answer.

The Democratic National Committee took these two questions and answers, had them printed up, and sent them all over the country as part of their campaign literature. It must have helped Kennedy's campaign against Nixon.

Ike's answers were not always so easy to understand. Even after hearing him answer a question at a press conference, I sometimes had to read a transcript (printed transcripts, provided to the press after news conferences, were another Eisenhower innovation) before I understood what he really said. At times, even a careful reading didn't help. Along with some other reporters, I compared Eisenhower's answers to the same question on oil and gas regulation and production over a period of eighteen months. Although he consistently gave the same answer, none of us could figure out what his position was, which side he was on. Both the oil men and the gasoline consumers felt he was on their side.

But on his good days, Dwight D. Eisenhower was capable of being a truly expressive leader and a real patriot, even at a presidential press conference. On days like that, I would come away from a press conference saying, "He was truly being president today."

# 4

# JFK: "I'm Not Scared of Sarah"

When John F. Kennedy was elected president, he announced to the print and broadcast media that presidential press conferences would be broadcast live. The networks were against the idea immediately. Preferring the security of taped broadcasts, which could be edited, and afraid of losing advertising revenue, ABC, CBS, and NBC bigwigs used scare tactics in their attempt to change Kennedy's mind. "Someday Sarah McClendon will ask you an embarrassing question in front of the whole country," they warned him.

"I know Sarah McClendon and she knows me," Kennedy told them, sticking to his guns, "and I'm not scared of her."

As it turned out, the networks were right. One of my questions was so embarrassing to Kennedy—I'll get back to that question presently—that the networks took the live press conference off the air. Of course, I didn't mean to embarrass Kennedy. My question dealt with a matter of national security that I felt needed his immediate attention. But by 1961, when Kennedy became president, the popularity of the televised presidential press conference had built up a large audience. People liked hearing the president being grilled. When sharp questions were asked on issues affecting people in their daily lives, they reacted by feeling as if they, too, were taking part. I know this is true because I received frequent letters, repeated comments, and tons of clippings. The comments from the public were usually more favorable than those from the editorial writers.

When Lyndon Johnson was vice-president, he told me during a private luncheon in the Capitol office of Senator Allen J. Ellender that my name was "a household word."

"A what?" I rejoined as we sat across the table from each other, scooping spoonfuls of hot Louisiana gumbo.

"I said it—your name is a household word in this country now."

I replied that I did not know what he was talking about. I thought, here's where I get the punch line.

"Know how I know that?" continued Lyndon. "The Kennedys took a poll and they found out."

I supposed this was done because the Kennedys wanted to know what effect questions and answers at his press conference were having on the public. I imagine they wanted to know if Kennedy had suffered from the question I had asked about Wieland and Miller in the State Department, although I asked it to alert Kennedy and remove risks. Maybe they wanted to know what issues were on people's minds. Until then, I had had no idea the Kennedys were all that public relations minded. Later, I began to see substantial proof of their quick reaction to public opinion in many ways.

I never really understood why I upset so many people. Perhaps I don't always present myself in the most flattering way. It is hard for me to sell myself; I can sell others better. I am a good public speaker, but, there again, I like to name names, dates, and places. Some people, like my friend Sally Champ, wife of a Canadian broadcaster, were really shocked at my exposure of public figures in a speech to women voters.

I'm still shy (although speaking up in public has become easier), and when I do force myself to question a president, my language may seem sharp. Perhaps my problem is that I prepare my own questions. Other reporters frequently ask questions supplied by their editors. My main "fault" seems to be that I dare to ask what other reporters are only thinking. I can't begin to count the times some other reporter told me he wished he had had the nerve to ask the question I had asked.

John Kennedy was never afraid to call on me, though. When some of my fellow reporters asked why he continued to take my questions, he told them he "couldn't help it." "I'm so curious about what she'll ask next," he explained, and he even went out of his way to call on me once after one of his press conferences had officially ended.

Kennedy's famous press conferences were held in the State Department auditorium, a room so large that it was difficult at times for a reporter to get recognized. Going against my usual pattern, I was too late that day to get a seat in front. I had not been recognized during the press conference, though I had tried my best, and I was on my feet trying to get recognized when the thirty-minute session came to an end. As the reporters started to file out, the president saw me and motioned for me to come down in front and ask my question. Although we were off the air, most of the reporters were still there and heard me ask him about a statement Adlai Stevenson had made on Red China that didn't jibe with Kennedy's own position. Would the president take steps in the future, I asked, to make certain that Stevenson's statements more closely coincided with his own?

Out loud, he said, "I should have just let this conference end."

Kennedy went on to say that he "didn't find anything to criticize," and added that he hoped for better coordination in the future. "With that vague and soft answer, I will leave you," said the president as he walked out the door. No one saw him flick me on the wrist, and no one heard when he whispered under his breath, "You and your soft little southern voice—!"

The next day, the Associated Press wrote: "President Kennedy upset tradition today when he responded to a woman reporter's question after his news conference had ended. But he indicated in his reply that he would have been at least as happy if he hadn't let the subject matter come up."

JFK had the best press of any president I covered. Kennedy worked hard to develop and maintain his ties with reporters and editors—something all public figures should consider doing. Reporters write about what they know, and JFK kept them well informed. Kennedy's good press, like everything else in government and in life, did not come by chance. The public believed the press courted the Kennedys; it was actually the Kennedys who courted the press.

Like other presidents, John Kennedy created media stars. Favored reporters were handed "scoops" directly from the Oval Office. He leaked to the *New York Herald Tribune* constantly. His pets—Charlie Bartlett, David Wise, Joe Kraft, Rowland Evans, Tom Ross, Ben Bradlee—mined Kennedy as if he were the mother lode. They cultivated his favors and friendship socially and professionally. Soon other government officials began to seek out these "in" reporters with more inside information. Party invitations flowed, which led to still more scoops.

Kennedy's favorites became quite snobbish about their valuable relations, and looked down their noses at less fortunate reporters. Of course, like most public officials, the Kennedys favored reporters who wrote for newspapers with a large circulation and an influential readership. Because my articles usually appear in small, regional newspapers, I have battled this prejudice through seven administrations, and it is still a problem in the eighth. Nixon's unhappy press secretary, Ron Ziegler, took me into his office and told me that if I had more readers I would have more clout. When Clark Mollenhoff was working as an adviser to Nixon, he told me that I could have brought about the reforms of Pentagon procedure on awarding big defense contracts which I had been fighting for if I worked for a newspaper with more impressive circulation figures.

I was trying to bring about a change in the way defense contracts worth millions of dollars were being handed out by a civilian who worked at the Pentagon. He was often seen around Washington being wined and dined by representatives of big corporations, and the awards he made seemed to me to reek of personal favoritism and wanton disregard of the taxpayers' money. He finally retired, but the situation has not changed enough to satisfy me.

(Actually, at the Pentagon, some of the civil servants manipulated the superiors, including at times the military officers, the top civilian appointees, and even the White House itself. Big decisions on contracts, I learned, were actually made by anonymous bureaucrats, then the decision for announcement was handed back to a particular branch of the service. The result was the top secretary or military officer became the scapegoat if that contract went sour and overcost the government, while the decision maker, the bureaucrat, went free of blame. There was a great amount of influence exerted on the methods of awarding these contracts by big defense contractors. I learned of a meeting at Ramey Air Force Base in Puerto Rico in the fall before Nixon took office. The purpose of the big contractors assembled and some visiting bureaucrats was to devise a method of keeping contract letting as it had been—to insure that the same biggies got the business.)

Some of Kennedy's favorite reporters were women. I knew Kennedy liked women and so, it seemed, did the networks and the wire services. Whenever a new president moves into the White House, the wire services and networks generally try to bring in a new crew to cover him. They try to give the plum White House assignment to a reporter who already knows and gets along with the new president.

Tony Vaccaro of the Associated Press staff in the Senate had played poker with former Senator Truman. Truman noticed Tony in the group of reporters outside his apartment house on the first morning he was driving to the White House to begin serving his term as president. He called Tony to come and ride with him. From that time on, Tony was the "in" man at the White House press room.

Lyndon Johnson found Bill Gill at the White House covering for ABC. Then the president discovered that he had known Bill's father on a ranch near Kingsville, Texas, and Johnson and Gill became fast friends.

Judy Woodruff had covered the Carters for some time in Plains. A Georgia girl, she knew how to get along with them. After the Carter victory, NBC assigned her to the White House to augment the network's staff. Ed Bradley of CBS also fit in well in the coverage of Carter: He was young, black, and became a close friend of Carter while covering the campaign. Naturally, CBS was glad to put him at the White House. Carter campaign coverage brought about a big turnover in reporters on wire services and networks.

The better a president likes a reporter, the better chance that reporter has of being assigned to cover the White House. The system also works in reverse. Reporters known to be feared or not liked by presidents may find themselves quickly transferred.

While Ron Nessen, then with NBC, denied it, I was told that Johnson did not like Elie Abel of NBC, who had covered President Kennedy, and supposedly helped to get Abel transferred elsewhere. And I was briefly transferred from two big papers in Texas, the *Austin American-Statesman* in the president's home area and the *Waco News-Tribune*, where I would have written much about Johnson, to two smaller papers, the *Lufkin Daily News* in the piney woods of deep eastern Texas, and the *Port Arthur News* at an outlying gulf port, where what happened to the latest oil tanker was more news than LBJ.

When a new crew arrives, the reporters who covered the outgoing president are usually devastated. No other assignment seems as prestigious and nationally important. When the Associated Press told Frances Lewine (who'd covered the White House for years) that she'd been reassigned to a consumer affairs beat, she quit and took a job in government public affairs with the huge Department of Transportation. (One of the reporters who'd covered Ford admitted to me that he was starting to enjoy Congress, his new assignment, although he was damned if he understood how it worked. Eventually he'll learn, and he'll also learn that Congress is where many of the best stories are.)

More women were assigned to cover Kennedy than had covered any president before him. One of these was Marianne Means. Marianne first met Kennedy while he was still a senator. He had made a speech in her hometown in Nebraska, where she worked on the local newspaper, and she was asked to drive him to the airport when he was ready to leave. The plane was late, and she stayed with him until he could board. They had a long talk and became friends. Marianne was a bright and beautiful woman, hard-working and a good reporter, and Kennedy was delighted with her. He told her that she was wasting her time in Nebraska, and that if she came to Washington, he would help her find a job. Soon after that, Marianne started working on the suburban Virginia newspaper that the Kennedys owned and ran with Clayton Fritchey. From there, she moved to the Hearst chain, and in 1960—her friendship with Kennedy surely being no handicap—she got the White House assignment.

Marianne was also one of Lyndon Johnson's favorites. When he became president, she saw him practically every day, and he encouraged her bosses at Hearst to let her become a syndicated columnist. Johnson used to apply his special brand of pressure to editors who didn't subscribe to the Means column (which didn't usually treat Johnson poorly), and I heard that some ended up taking the column rather than saying no to LBJ.

Poor Lyndon never had a prayer in his campaign against Jack Kennedy. At the Democratic National Convention in 1960, I remember my friend and fellow Texan Lyndon Johnson shaking a finger at me when he and Kennedy were rivals for the presidential nomination. "Sarah," he said, "sometimes I think you are for Kennedy." I couldn't answer him because, although I felt a certain loyalty to Johnson, Kennedy appealed to me just as he appealed to the rest of the American public. I liked Jack Kennedy very much. I also loved the Kennedy family. And until Jimmy Carter came along, he had the most effective political organization I'd ever seen.

The Kennedys had an office full of political professionals and volunteers working for at least two years before he ran for president. The office was about a block from the Capitol. The Kennedy family, especially Papa Joe, was very influential, very smart, and very good at organizing. By the time individual state organizations had to name delegates to the national convention, the Kennedy people were clearly in control and got the nod. LBJ could never fight that. He started too late. I accompanied Johnson on a campaign trip to Colorado and saw it with my own eyes. Colorado's top politicians, including the governor, all attended a party in Johnson's honor. They were friendly and polite to Johnson, but they couldn't help him—they were already committed to Kennedy.

During the campaign, in the fall of 1960, I accompanied Mrs. Johnson and Eunice Kennedy Shriver, Ethel Kennedy, and others of the Kennedy women on a campaign trip through the Southwest. We ended up at the Johnson ranch in the Texas hill country, where we played touch football, went swimming, and put on skits about ourselves and the trip. One hot afternoon, while we were sitting by the swimming pool, all of us fully dressed, Eunice Kennedy Shriver (who I have always thought to be the smartest member of the clan) suddenly leaned back and deliberately slid into the water. After she had been swimming for a few minutes, she realized she was wearing a new dress that was not washable. "Too late now," she said and kept swimming. I noticed that she was wearing a diamond as big as a bird's egg.

I remember another trip with the Kennedys in 1962, a

fantastic trip to Mexico City with President and Mrs. Kennedy, who spoke Spanish to the delight of the crowds. The city was decorated as if it were Mardi Gras, and there were huge red and green posters everywhere advertising Mexico's only political party. The streets were so crowded that I was once pushed against a wire fence and almost had my dress ripped off and I lost my purse.

One night in Mexico City, I was one of the pool reporters* assigned to cover a dinner reception for President and Mrs. Kennedy being given by the minister for external affairs, Manuel Tellos, and his wife. Tellos had been the Mexican ambassador to the United States, and he and his wife had once been my guests at a Women's Press Club dinner.

The crowd at the reception was so large that people were fainting. I heard that Marianne Means had become ill and had gone back to her hotel. Many other reporters also left when they were told, as I was told, that it would be impossible to gain admission to the room where the president was having dinner. But you could never tell when a president might make big news. I wouldn't leave without seeing the Kennedys and the Telloses, so I used my special technique of plowing through a crowd.

First I used one elbow to slip in a little bit, then I used the other elbow to slip in a little bit. I wormed my way through in a zigzag pattern, two or three inches at a time. Finally, only a door separated me from the official party. When that door opened, my only line of vision into the room was under the arm of the man in front of me. I

---

* At times when the entire group of reporters traveling with a president cannot or need not be with him, one or two reporters (we all take turns) cover an event for the rest of the group. These pool reporters type up a story, describing everything that happened, so that the rest of the reporters can file a story as if they'd been there.

looked under his arm, and there, looking back at me, was John F. Kennedy, who was seated facing the door. It was amazing that he saw me and even more amazing when he asked, "Isn't that Sarah McClendon out there? Bring her in here."

When the rest of the crowd realized that I was to be allowed into the room, they pushed so hard to get to the space I was vacating that I was literally projected into the middle of the room, like a bomb. There I stood, right in front of the head table, out of breath and looking bug-eyed. Suddenly, we all laughed. I felt a little foolish, but I was delighted to be inside and quickly started to get my story. Later, when I filed my pool report, I found out that I was the only reporter who managed to get near the Kennedys that night.

Back in Washington, it was at one of Kennedy's press conferences that I asked what I consider to be one of the most important questions I ever asked a public official, the question that was so embarrassing to Kennedy that, at first, all the networks took the conference off the air. My question, and the story that followed, began for me in late 1960, when Edward Harrigan, a young lawyer I knew, called to say that he was bringing a lawyer from Miami to my house that night on A Street, SE, on Capitol Hill. That was my introduction to what was to become a long and involved chapter in my life. It was to result in several years of study and in one of the worst experiences a reporter (or a president) ever had because of a news story.

Harrigan, who had previously served in naval intelligence, had, in the past, come up with many interesting story suggestions for me. This time he brought me William Otis Fuller, a former resident of Havana, whose son Bobby, a marine, had just been put to death by Castro in Cuba. Mr. Fuller was a gentle, quiet man who, despite his grief, seemed calm and truthful. During the course of our conversation, Fuller mentioned that William Wieland, the State Department's director of Caribbean affairs, had just lost his job. I considered myself something of an authority on the Caribbean and on this particular area of coverage at the State Department, yet the information about Wieland was news to me. The next day I checked at the State Department, where I found that, although it was true that Wieland was leaving his job, there had been no public announcement of this action. When I realized that Fuller was telling me news before it happened, I concluded that he was getting his information from the Cuban underground based in Miami, and that the Cubans were very close to at least one avenue leading to the decision-making process of our State Department.

Fuller also told me that Wieland had known for a long time that Castro was a Communist, but that he had never told this to his superiors at the State Department. I was becoming very interested in William Wieland, and when I studied his career, I found that he had climbed up the State Department ladder amazingly quickly, with a record of being at strategic places with important people at the right time. I began to watch Wieland's friends, too, from the small group of newsmen with whom he regularly played poker and exchanged information to his superior at the State Department, Richard Rubottom, a Texan, who seemed overly dependent on Wieland for advice.

There are many mysteries about the State Department that no one seems to be able to solve. To me, the State Department has always been a government within the government, a government which is independent of administrations that come and go with their elected and appointed officials. The State Department has a hierarchy of its own, and it is very difficult to know at any time who is really in charge. I have talked about this with several long-term career officers of the State Department and they agree.

In the course of my research, I discovered that Wieland was under intensive investigation by the Senate Judiciary Subcommittee on Internal Security. He was later assigned to work with J. Clayton Miller, a State Department analyst, whose name had appeared in the investigative files of the House Un-American Activities Committee in connection with membership in several organizations in which the committee was interested. Wieland and Miller were assigned to the Office of Management of the State Department, where they were put to work reorganizing the department. In such positions both men could have access to the government's intelligence files, which contained the names of United States spies and agents throughout the world (so I was told by officials with more background in the State Department's organization than I had).

I was quite surprised that this post came to Wieland. I had been following him for sixteen months. During that time, many others in the State Department began to have some fear about his trustworthiness, for nearly every time Wieland's friends—and he had strong ones—would get him in line for an interesting new assignment or overseas post, he would get pulled back. Once he was detained for language training. I was told that Bobby Kennedy had seen to it that he was kept from going to those new, sensitive posts. From what I learned, Bobby must have been tailing Wieland.

After months of watching, I was all but catapulted into asking the question about Wieland and Miller by fast-moving events in the Senate Judiciary Subcommittee on Internal Security. After I had decided to ask the question, I kept trying to find out more about the new jobs of these two men and was on the telephone in an anteroom of the State Department auditorium until the last two minutes before the conference started. I had already been inside and put a hold on a good seat down front, then went out to do more telephoning.

When the president recognized me, the questioning went like this:

McClendon: Mr. President, Sir, two well-known security risks have recently been put on a task force in the State Department to help organize the Office of Management.

Kennedy: Well, now, who?

McClendon: William Arthur Wieland . . .

Kennedy: You are—the thing—I think that—would you give me the other name?

McClendon: Yes, Sir, J. Clayton Miller.

Kennedy: Right, well now, I don't—I think the term— I would say that the term you've used to describe them is a very strong term which I think you should be prepared to substantiate. I'm familiar with Mr. Miller's record because I happened to look at it the other day. He has been cleared by the State Department. In my opinion, he's fit for the duties which he's carrying out. Mr. Rusk and I both looked into the matter, so therefore I cannot accept your description of him.

McClendon: Did you look at Mr. William Arthur Wieland, too?

Kennedy: We—I'm familiar with Mr. Wieland. I'm also familiar with his duties at the present time, and in my opinion Mr. Miller and Mr. Wieland—the duties they've been assigned to, they can carry out without detriment to the interests of the United States, and, I hope, without detriment to their characters by your question.

At that point, apparently, Pierre Salinger, Kennedy's press secretary, gave the signal for his boss to get out of there, and the press conference ended five minutes ahead of schedule. According to the story in the *Herald Tribune* the next day, Sarah McClendon "was surrounded by reporters with questions for her when the conference ended, but declined to give the grounds on which she based her question, adding that she had her own confidential sources."

Reaction to my question was immediate and bad. The Wieland story was big—any story concerning national security is big—and I had done something most reporters never did: I named names. And not only was I airing the State Department's dirty linen in public, but I had committed the worst sin of all—I had embarrassed Jack Kennedy. I took an awful lot of abuse, personally and professionally, after I asked Kennedy about Wieland and Miller. A typical reaction came from the late Congressman John Rooney, a New York Democrat, whom I had counted as a friend. "I used to give you stories to help you out," he told me in disgust, "but how can I help you now? I can't be seen talking to you." The late Representative Francis Walter, a Pennsylvania Democrat for whom Kennedy had made a speech during Walter's re-election bid, said he could no longer help me verify information through files of the House Un-American Activities Committee, which he chaired.

I started getting phone calls and letters from all parts of the country. The mail had to be delivered by truck, and I had to hire volunteers just to help me read it all. I developed a following among the extreme right wing, who thought I was one of them, and among the expatriate Cubans, who saw in me a new champion. And I found that I had become the subject of newspaper stories myself. The *New York Herald Tribune* described me as a "gadfly" at presidential press conferences (which I took as an insult despite the fact that a gadfly, according to my dictionary, is "habitually engaged in provocative criticism of existing situations"). But I hate the word *gadfly* and felt my work was far more important. *Time* magazine accused me of being "a president baiter" who set a trap for Kennedy with my question on Wieland and Miller.

Almost everyone had an opinion on the question, and most opinions were bad. Bobby Kennedy, then the attorney general, let it be known that he planned to make an official inquiry as to how far a reporter could go when questioning a president, a potential threat he never carried out. The State Department held a press conference of its own immediately after the president's press conference ended (which I was tipped off about and attended and where State Department employees threatened to sue for libel any reporters who mentioned Wieland's or Miller's name in their stories). The State Department counsel, Abe Chayes, told reporters once that the State Department considered suing me, but they were advised that even more publicity would be the result of such a suit, and that I didn't have money to pay a judgment anyway.

The Women's National Press Club announced a program on How Far a Reporter Could Go When Questioning a President. Obviously, the program was aimed at me—no one else asked questions like mine. Bonnie Angelo, now a Washington correspondent for *Time* magazine, arranged the program, but only one of her guest speakers showed up: Louis Nizer, the famous libel lawyer from New York. I showed up, too—I felt I was required to attend, although I found it both distasteful and inappropriate for a group of reporters to place limits on their own freedom of inquiry.

I remember the evening as nothing less than Sarah McClendon on trial, but Angelo neglected to supply me with a defense lawyer.

On the other hand, I felt I could have sued some of the newspapers that printed negative editorials about me. Most of the anti-McClendon criticism appeared in newspapers, especially the more liberal newspapers. Many of my critics knew nothing about my question or Wieland (and not much about me, either, although some of them thought they did). I was not out to create a scandal about Wieland or Miller personally, but as a reporter and a citizen, I believe I have the right to name names when my facts indicate national security is involved.

After a long investigation of Wieland's activities and personal life, the Senate Subcommittee on Internal Security was due to release a security report on him within a few days of the press conference. Secretary of State Dean Rusk went to see Senator James Eastland, a Democrat from Mississippi and chairman of the parent committee—Senate Judiciary. Rusk was given information about what possibly would be in any report to be issued and found it to be adverse to the State Department's claim of innocence on Wieland's part. Then Rusk asked Eastland to delay the report. Eastland, glad to play along with the Kennedy administration for possible future favors, held it up until October 16, 1962.

It had been obvious to me that the Kennedys knew about Wieland's questionable record all along, since Wieland was finally pushed out of his prestigious job at the State Department after Castro came to power in Cuba. Bobby personally took an interest in what remained of Wieland's career, and Wieland's final days at the State Department were spent in a series of nonsensitive posts. Years later, Roger Jones, deputy assistant secretary for management at the State Department, who lost his job following my question on Wieland and Miller, approached me at a luncheon in Washington to say, much to my surprise, "I want to shake your hand. Because of you, we found out about a lot of things we never knew were going on in government."

I loved that. Mission accomplished.

Luckily, the Wieland incident has not completely clouded my memories of the Kennedy administration, and I can remember Kennedy himself with the greatest fondness. One of my most prized possessions is a letter he wrote to me in his own handwriting, which I keep in my files. (Apparently I had sent him a column I had written.) It reads:

Sarah,

I would not want to comment on the syntax and sentence structure of your column in the *El Paso Times*. But I will say that the girl they used as your stand-in for the photograph is a pip of a woman. Indeed she is—verily.

JFK

# 5

## JFK's Unfinished Business

Shock is a funny thing. I was surprised how deeply President Kennedy's death affected the personal lives of people who had not been close to him. I never realized how much he meant to me personally. Although I didn't agree with him on many issues, I found I felt about him in death as if he were the boy down the street, my neighbor's son. I was never intimately acquainted with him, but I did know him and I adored him. I never really understood him, though. He ran too fast for me, something I used to criticize him for. He did not complete one program befort starting two others. Perhaps he had a premonition of death. He was a young man with, oh, so much to do. He introduced government programs like a man fighting for time.

I had had numerous brief but personal encounters with President Kennedy. When he was a senator, he would stop me in the Capitol and ask, "How is your daughter?" which of course pleased me much. During the campaign, he could not understand why shortage of travel funds prevented me from traveling with him. Once he saw me in the large crowd at Washington National Airport just before he was leaving on his plane, the *Caroline*, and came up to me to say, "Aren't you going with us?"

It was much like that when he came out of his White House office the last time to fly to Texas. He was in a hurry, as usual. He turned swiftly to the right to walk to the helicopter, but something caught his eye and he quickly wheeled and spotted me and another reporter standing on the porch steps outside the Oval Office to see him off. He smiled and gave a quick wave of the hand as if he understood that I would not be going. It was the last time I was to see him alive, his last gesture at the White House.

Of course, as a reporter from Texas, I was involved in the president's last trip, even if I did not go along. The newspapers I wrote for had their own reporters in Texas. My job was to find out about preparations for the trip, which were being made in Washington. Try as I might, I couldn't get the route the president and his party would follow through the streets of San Antonio and Houston. Yet the motorcade route through Dallas had been given out to the press two days before. Felton West, a reporter from the *Houston Post*, and I stood before Press Secretary Salinger in his office in the White House the day before the trip. We told him that our editors were begging to publish the parade routes in their papers so that their readers could make plans to watch the parade. I told Salinger that I was sure that the president would appreciate the presence of a cheering throng, and that such throngs did not just appear by chance. Wasn't voter appeal the purpose of the trip? We had been trying to get this information for days, and here we were at the end of the timetable. Still, Salinger did not give us the routes. He didn't even give us a reason. In frustration, I lashed out at Salinger, saying, "Then you can take your bloody trip for all I care. . . ." Salinger looked belligerent, and his secretary motioned for me to leave the room.

After Kennedy's death, I went to Salinger and apologized tearfully for my use of that term. "I know, Sarah, I know," he comforted me.

Salinger was superb during those days. He took over many of the arrangements and announcements, and answered the reporters' many questions. So many of us gathered at the White House to hear what sad news he had to give us that the press briefings had to be moved from Salinger's office to the big lobby in the West Wing of the White House.

I first heard the news that Kennedy had been shot while I was working in my office at home. In December, 1963, I wrote:

"My woman's intuition tells me that Lee Harvey Oswald could not and did not do that by himself. He was just a diversion. It could have been the work of the underworld, using Oswald, with his peculiar background, as a smoke screen, or it could have been a national or an international plot. I think there should be a fund devoted to finding out the truth. I always had the feeling Kennedy might die in office, but I thought it would be the result of one of his chronic ailments."


I'll never forget seeing the casket carrying the body of John F. Kennedy when it was brought home from Dallas. Late that afternoon, the afternoon of November 22, 1963, I had driven over to Georgetown University to pick up my daughter, Sally, who was a student there. She was crying softly when she got into the car. We decided she should accompany me to the airport to be there when the body arrived. We drove twenty miles to Andrews Air Force Base, where *Air Force One* was due to land. The Lord must have guided us as we got close to the base because, although we were not familiar with the complicated route, we drove directly to the terminal. At the entrance I was afraid the Secret Service would not permit Sally to enter, but they knew me and when they saw my White House pass, they lifted the ropes for her, too.

We arrived a few minutes before the plane carrying the body landed. The airport was full of congressmen, officials, diplomats, and newspaper reporters. I'm sure none of us who was there will ever forget the sight of Mrs. Kennedy, her clothing stained with her husband's blood. Evelyn Lincoln, Kennedy's secretary, was immaculate in a black velvet coat and spotless white gloves. The contrast was striking.

When Mrs. Kennedy climbed into the front seat of the gray navy hearse to ride along with her husband's body to Bethesda Naval Hospital for the autopsy, I found myself thinking that I would have done the same thing.

The new president, Lyndon Baines Johnson, and his wife, Lady Bird, left *Air Force One* after Mrs. Kennedy had driven away. The two came down the ramp arm in arm. They wore sober, sad expressions. He shook a few hands and accepted the sympathy and best wishes of Speaker John W. McCormack, suddenly the second most powerful man in the United States. Then Mr. Johnson turned to shake hands with the crowd of diplomats from nearly every country in the world—all except Russia. "This is a sad occasion," I heard the ambassador from Germany say, "for your country and mine." Cries of "Lyndon, so sorry" came from a crowd of senators and congressmen who swarmed around him. Many Republicans were present. Senator George Aiken from Vermont, who rarely went out at night, was there, patting Johnson's chest familiarly and fondly while expressing his deep grief. Aiken and Kennedy had liked each other. Senator Everett Dirksen from Illinois, Republican minority leader of the Senate, was there, as was Senator Hubert Humphrey of Minnesota and his wife, Muriel. Although many senators and congressmen had not supported Kennedy and had not felt close to him, they were all joined in grief. I was numb from shock. I had a deep sense of loss from both a public and private standpoint. I also felt so frustrated for my country.

The only time I saw even a half-smile on Lyndon Johnson's face was when he shook hands with my daughter, whom he liked very much and who was a friend of his daughter Lynda.

Finally, Rufus Youngblood, the Secret Service agent whom I knew well from my travels with Johnson and who had covered Johnson's body with his own that afternoon in Dallas, checked the microphone and motioned for the new president to speak. After a few short, sad words, Johnson went to the Executive Office next to the White House, and sat down and wrote a letter to Jack Kennedy's children.

But it was time for me to go to work. From years of covering oil field fires, car accidents, murders, and hurricanes, I knew how to put my emotions aside and get the quotes.

I talked to three Texas congressmen who had flown back to Washington that night with Kennedy's body and with the new president. "It was awful, terrible," said Democrat Albert Thomas of Houston. None of the three could really talk. Words did not come easily. "This was a horrible crime," said Homer Thornberry, Democrat from Austin, who had planned to go on to El Paso that night but returned to Washington instead. "Were you close to him when he was shot?" I asked Jack Brooks of Beaumont. "Pretty close," he said, and then grimaced in the agony of recalling that moment. "The first thing I thought of was Puerto Rico," added Thomas, who had been on the floor of the House of Representatives on the day in 1954 I had watched a group of Puerto Ricans shoot into a a crowd of congressmen from the gallery. "I heard boom, boom, and then later another boom," Thomas said. "I shall never forget that sound."

I interviewed Senator Ralph Yarborough, another Texas Democrat, who flew in on a plane that followed *Air Force One*. In all, nine Texas officials were on the two planes. Yarborough, still in a state of shock, walked slowly. His eyes were dilated and he was speechless at first. Some of his companions were crying and so were their wives. Yarborough had been riding in the third car of the motorcade with Vice-President and Mrs. Johnson. When they heard the shots, they followed the Secret Service's command to get down. They didn't know what had happened or where they were going until they arrived at the hospital. Yarborough watched Kennedy being taken out of the car and spoke to Mrs. Kennedy, but he would not repeat their conversation. According to Yarborough, just before the shooting "the president was in good spirits and full of enthusiasm. Mrs. Kennedy appeared to be enjoying the trip very much. It was the biggest crowd I have ever seen in Dallas. Bigger than the crowd for Astronaut Cooper. If this hadn't happened, I believe that the president would have been seen by one million people that day, one tenth of the population of Texas."

Another reporter asked Yarborough whether he thought the murder had been the work of a radical rightist. Without being briefed on news developments, Yarborough replied,

"It is an outgrowth of a campaign of hate. I think the whole world will feel this loss for years to come. This is the saddest day I've ever known in American history."

The entire nation was devastated.

At home, my daughter was literally sick with grief. For days, like most of the country, she sat in front of the television, scarcely moving. I began to fear that she would never come out of it. To her and to other young people, Kennedy had been the only leader they had felt close to. They now felt alone, abandoned, shattered.

Funeral plans were quickly made. Charles de Gaulle of France, Prince Philip of England, Queen Wilhelmina of the Netherlands, and many other dignitaries planned to attend. But, as a reporter who covered the Texas-Mexico border, I was amazed to discover that no one from Mexico was on the list of mourners. I was also aware that immediately after Kennedy was shot the Mexican border was closed to all traffic. The Mexican people loved Kennedy— it was easy to remember the crowds who had gathered to see him in Mexico City. When the Mexican government finally announced it would send a representative, it was among the last to do so.

When the body of President Kennedy was removed from the White House to be taken to the rotunda of the Capitol to lie in state, I and other members of the press fell in behind the other dignitaries and walked behind the body down Pennsylvania Avenue. I do not think any of us had planned it. We just kept on. En route we were joined by other friends and supporters who had known and worked with Kennedy. For most of the walk, I marched beside a couple whose names I never learned. From their conversation I found out that he had worked for the president, and that she, along with other Kennedy friends, had spent the night at the Library of Congress, researching the funerals of Abraham Lincoln and others at Mrs. Kennedy's request. This research was typical of the Kennedys' organization, and Mrs. Kennedy was highly praised for her part in planning the funeral services.

Mrs. Kennedy's outpouring of affection for her wounded husband in Dallas was immediate and spontaneous. Pictures show her standing over him in an attempt to shield his body from more bullets, then cradling his body in her arms. Representative Henry Gonzales of Texas, who saw her sitting in the emergency ward outside the operating room in Dallas, her gloves, her suit, and her stockings coagulated with blood, said that he had never seen "a more pitiable, desolate, lonely figure."

Mrs. Kennedy saw to it that her two small children had a chance to participate in the memory and the history of those moments. After all, it was part of their heritage. They said good-bye to their father at two Masses in the East Room, then drove with their mother to the public ceremony in the rotunda of the Capitol. Mrs. Kennedy had apparently rehearsed Caroline and John-John well. John-John was three years old on the day his father was buried.

I'll never forget that day. Reporters could either go to St. Matthew's Cathedral for the Mass or to Arlington National Cemetery; time and the processional would not permit both. I chose the cemetery, where I had a place high up but directly over the burial plot.

I recall I wore a black dress, black lace veil, and black gloves. Later I heard Betty Beale, a society columnist who liked things to be proper, say that I was the only reporter who was properly dressed. What nonsense! I had never thought about propriety when I dressed for the funeral. I wore that outfit because I felt sorrow.

Following the lighting of the Eternal Flame—an idea of

Jackie's that she put into effect without asking the permission of Congress, the Army Engineers, or the Commission on Fine Arts—the funeral party broke up to attend two receptions. Jackie received the princes and potentates at the White House, and she took time to speak privately with each one of them. They marveled at her strength—so did I. Another person might have gone into seclusion after the funeral. Jackie, who had always seemed so shy and so fragile, surprised us all.

The new president and Mrs. Johnson received the foreign dignitaries at the State Department. As they filed by, they seemed anxious to meet and talk with Johnson but they did not tarry long. After the funeral, there was another reception at the Soviet Embassy for Anastas Mikoyan, who had come from Russia for the sad occasion. Eleven men had been assigned by our government to act as his guards. Three of these guards were men who worked for our own State Department, and later, at the reception, they noticed that each American present was surrounded by Russians. And although everyone was guarded and careful about what was said, one of the Russians present seemed so overwhelmed with grief over Kennedy's death that he said to one of the Americans, "Look behind the man Ruby. Find out who he is. Your government must find out who he is."

"Do you think he was working for another country?" asked the American. But the Russian just shrugged his shoulders and walked away.

Throughout the years since Kennedy's death, the identity of the assassin has intrigued the people of the world—the Russians, the Americans, and almost everyone else. Perhaps it is because of their own experience with governmental plotting and assassination, but the subject has never ceased to interest the Russians.

The death of Jack Ruby left Waggoner Carr, the attorney general of Texas, one of the most frustrated men in public life. Carr had wanted to give Ruby a lie detector test, but was told that such a test would be impossible due to Ruby's cancerous condition. Carr kept asking for the test until Ruby died.

Carr was equally frustrated in his other efforts to get to the bottom of the Kennedy assassination. He was determined to give the state of Texas its own investigation of the murder. Carr went to Washington with Leon Jaworski, the Houston attorney who later became the Watergate special prosecutor; Robert G. Storey, a Dallas attorney; and others to prepare for this investigation. I called Jaworski at the Mayflower Hotel the night the lawyers got to Washington. I had heard that the government planned its own investigation, and I wondered how this would affect the Texans' plans. Jaworski assured me at 11:45 that evening that the Texans would conduct their own investigation, regardless of what others might do. But by 9:30 the next morning, the Texas investigation was out of business. Another Texan had doomed it—Lyndon Johnson. Jaworski, Carr, and the others were sick, embarrassed, and frustrated as they had to announce at a press conference at the Justice Department that the Warren Commission alone would look into the case. It was easy to see that these men had not made the decision.

But later, as testimony was taken, Carr and other Texans were amazed to see that the Warren Commission refused to take the word of Governor John Connally, who had been riding in the car with the murdered president and who, because of his own wounds, should have been able to best remember the path of the bullets. Despite this, however, Connally himself lashed out later in a public press conference at those who wanted to discredit the Warren Commission and reopen the investigation.

Lyndon Johnson, who thrived on secrecy, who never believed in making the American public a partner in the inner workings of government, and who did not trust the press, contrived with the grief-stricken Kennedys to keep much of the Warren Commission material secret for seventy-five years.

This secrecy set off a cult of investigation that involved college students, government and congressional attorneys, private investigators, public interest attorneys, newsmen, and former agents of the Central Intelligence Agency. This cult operated feverishly in the sixties and seventies, and will probably continue to operate until we get some answers. I have a collector's item in my library—an autographed copy of *Portrait of the Assassin* by Congressman Gerald R. Ford, a member of the Warren Commission. Ford was a strong supporter of the one-assassin theory, with Oswald as the culprit. It is interesting reading.

I find it ironic indeed that this great country, so advanced in technology, resources, and talent, cannot solve the mysteries of who killed Jack Kennedy; why and exactly how Martin Luther King was killed; what motivated the death of Bobby Kennedy as well as the shooting of George Wallace. I know that solutions to all this must be possible. For a canny, bright people not to find solutions smacks of childishness, abject neglect, or the manipulations of some person or group seeking deliberate avoidance for a special interest.

Were the assassinations and attempts at assassination one-man schemes or broad conspiracies by nuts, the International Crime Syndicate, members of the Mafia (who were pressed into service as part of wider bargaining), the CIA, organized gambling interests (which were fast becoming victims of Kennedy law enforcement), right-wing ideologists, or some foreign intrigue?

Solutions to these malignant problems, still gnawing at our civilization, must be found, I believe, before we can get on with our task as Jack Kennedy saw it. Robert Kennedy summarized it as follows in a memorial to the president: ". . . We have the capacity to make this the best generation in the history of mankind or make it the last. If we do our duty, if we meet our responsibilities and our obligations, not just as Democrats but as American citizens in our local cities and towns and farms, in our states and in the country as a whole, then this country is going to be the best generation in the history of mankind. . . ."

# 6

## LBJ Manages the News

When Senator Lyndon B. Johnson accepted Senator John F. Kennedy's invitation to speak at Faneuil Hall in Boston, he invited me to go along on the trip. I was covering Lyndon closely and carefully in those days for the *San Antonio Light*, the *Austin American-Statesman*, the *El Paso Times*, the *Waco News-Tribune*, and several other Texas newspapers as their Washington correspondent.

An airplane ride with Johnson meant hours of fascinating listening for me. LBJ was a master storyteller and a non-stop talker who craved an audience, especially on an airplane. He was also a good politician, and he knew that it was important for the folks down in Texas to read my stories describing the important work Johnson was doing for them up North.

We traveled from Washington to Boston in a small plane supplied by the Westinghouse Corporation. It was not unusual then, as it is not unusual now, for public figures to travel all over the country in planes provided by large corporations. Although Lyndon and I disagreed about the morality of this kind of travel (even when Lyndon leased his own plane, he did it through one of his businesses), the trip was free and I would have been a damn jackass if I hadn't gone. It was a great chance to pick up a story.

After the speech, the Johnsons went to a hotel suite to freshen up and change clothes and to meet and greet Boston's top politicians. I remember meeting at least a dozen judges, state legislators, city officials, and prominent citizens in the crowded reception room. Lesser politicians were lined up in the corridor just outside the suite, waiting for a glimpse of the great man. I was the only reporter present. Lady Bird had a problem with her dress and needed a needle and thread. The room telephones were tied up. When I opened the door of the suite to summon the hotel housekeeper, the Boston politicos passed the word down the line, as if in a comic opera: "A maid, a maid for Lady Bird."

The comic opera had its second act when Jack Kennedy decided on the spur of the moment to fly back to Washington with the Johnson party. The always-willing inner circle of JFK volunteers sent the word to the troops: "Jack needs his luggage . . . Jack needs it now . . . Quick, get Jack's luggage."

Flying back that night while Lady Bird caught up on some much-needed sleep in the front of the plane, the rest of us sat in the back in a circle and talked. The subject of our conversation was politics, of course, and there was lots of first-rate, behind-the-scenes Senate gossip, something both Kennedy and Johnson loved. A reporter can find out a lot on a trip like this one—everyone gets very close, very friendly on an airplane—and though the two senators did most of the talking, I felt so at home with them that when there was a lull in the conversation I spoke up.

"You two would make a really great team," I said. There was dead silence. No one said a word. But I could tell they were both thinking the same thing: Who would be at the top of a presidential ticket and who would be number two? That was in April, 1959. Two persons who overheard this, Claude Hobbs of Westinghouse Broadcasting and O. B. Lloyd of LBJ's staff, have frequently recalled the conversation to me in recent years.

Although Lyndon never had a prayer against Jack Kennedy, he was still a fascinating man, and became a legend in Texas and Washington political annals long before he reached the White House. He was an amazing specimen of vitality, eager to serve the public and possessed of an iron will. His idiosyncrasies were not faults so much as they were part of his drive to attain his one goal: to serve his country.

But here I am analyzing Johnson when the thing he hated most was being analyzed. He was too sensitive for that, and his sensitivities were part of his general insecurity. LBJ had a real inferiority complex all his life, built-in from an early life of poverty. After a childhood spent on a Texas farming frontier, a childhood lacking in educational and cultural advantages, Lyndon was hungry for money, power, and security. And what Lyndon wanted Lyndon usually got.

Although he drove his staff with a constant fury and although he frequently frustrated the media to the breaking point, Lyndon was truly a man of accomplishment. I always thought it would have been interesting to see what he might have done had he not been driven from office by the Vietnam War.

Lyndon Johnson often used the phrase "he is a can do man." Woe be it to any other kind who crossed his path. A manual of the "can do" cult, as taught by Johnson, ought to be placed in every bureaucrat's Welcome Wagon kit when he first arrives in Washington. Lyndon hated red tape, "going through channels" (the federal government could save billions of dollars if it eliminated channels), and endless delay. He was interested in results, and used any method that worked to get things *done.* The concept of the impossible was totally lacking in his mentality. This "can do" spirit was totally lacking in successive administrations until Jimmy Carter revived it.

One of Johnson's most trusty weapons in his war to get things done was his own power of persuasion. Jack Bell, the Associated Press correspondent who covered the Senate for many years, called it "the Johnson treatment," and few could resist once it was applied. Many years ago, Lyndon used the Johnson treatment on the owners of a radio station in Austin on which he had his eye. The station was not on the market. As a matter of fact, the owners had never thought about selling, but after one full weekend of Johnson's proposals, deals, pleas, arguments, and persuasion, according to Johnson, they gave in to his persistence and sold.

What Johnson said was undoubtedly true but a series of events set the stage for the turnover in ownership and made the atmosphere just right for Johnson to acquire the radio station, KTBC at Austin.

As a result, the station that its owner, the late Dr. J. G. Ulmer, had figured to be worth $1 million, went for around $15,000.

It was not bought with $10,000 from Alabama farmlands, as local gossip had it. Among the Johnson assets was $27,000 of promissory notes that Lady Bird obtained from her father, T. J. Taylor, a Karnack, Texas, storekeeper, as a result of dividing up her mother's estate in Texas. Most of the property had already gone to her two brothers. The father was not wealthy, but he owned the store and 11,000 acres of land in Harrison County.

At the time, radio management was in its infancy in Texas. It was being pioneered by Dr. Ulmer, a Yale graduate and a sometime preacher who owned the radio stations in Tyler and Austin and other cities, and with whom I was well acquainted. He had some devoted fans, and many enemies who did not understand what he was trying to do and therefore distrusted him. His lack of political backing and clout doubtless contributed to what happened to him at the Federal Communications Commission in Washington, which in turn contributed in a major way to his having to sell the Austin station at a low price.

Dr. Ulmer was having a hard time making a go of the station in Austin and seriously considered selling out to Texas millionaire Jim West, who did not like the way the federal government was performing in the world of Franklin D. Roosevelt. West dreamed of building a communications network to air his views and "save the country"; the Austin station quickly became involved in a controversy over conservative versus liberal views.

Dr. Ulmer agreed to sell to West, subject to approval, of course, of the FCC. While they were awaiting approval, World War II came on and West began to waver in his plan.

About this time, President Roosevelt named James Lawrence Fly of Dallas to become chairman of the FCC. Then Dr. Ulmer heard a radio broadcast saying that the FCC had revoked the licenses of the several radio stations he owned, claiming "hidden ownership," which was contrary to FCC rules. Ulmer could not imagine what was happening. He had had on record several partners in the Austin enterprise.

The FCC let Ulmer continue to operate the Austin station but kept him so busy attending hearings and giving testimony that he could not give it much personal supervision, and the station's financial situation began to deteriorate alarmingly. If only the FCC would let him complete the sale to Jim West!

Ulmer sought out a politically knowledgeable attorney for help. He asked State Senator Alvin J. Wirtz of Austin to take the case and represent him before the FCC. Wirtz demurred. Then Wirtz told Ulmer that he could not take the case. He had gone to Washington. There, Wirtz, a close friend and political associate of Representative Lyndon Johnson, told Johnson all about the station's plight.

Finally, West died. The West estate said it had no claim. Lady Bird filed for application to purchase. Then the job of whittling down the price further with Ulmer began.

After the Johnsons began operating the radio station, they had little difficulty acquiring the first TV permit in Austin. Thus began their monopoly and their fortune. This station became the source of great wealth and power for Johnson and his family in later years. The story that it was Lady Bird's station, which she bought with a $10,000 inheritance and ran herself, was one of the myths Johnson created about himself. She did go over the books regularly with a management team in Austin, however, and signed the checks.

I was able to observe "can do-ism" in action when Judge Woodrow Bean of El Paso, a "can do" man like Johnson, came to Washington to seek LBJ's help. Johnson was in the Senate then, and I was covering Washington for the *El Paso Times*. When a county judge comes to Washington to see his senator, that's news in El Paso. Judge Bean's problem was the Cordova Island Bridge between Mexico and Texas, which had been uncompleted and useless for years. Neither country seemed capable of winding up negotiations. Johnson said he'd help, and asked to see a representative from every possible agency involved: the State Department, the Border Patrol, the International Boundary and Water Commission, Immigration, Customs, the Federal Highway Administration, and the Department of Agriculture. The men met in Johnson's third-floor office in the Capitol, and I sat in on the meeting and watched Johnson put each man on the spot.

"Why isn't the work finished?" he asked, and the bureaucrats began to waffle and give excuses and blame one another until they realized Lyndon was not going to let them get away with that. It became increasingly clear to these men (and to me) that they would actually have to *do* something. As the facts came out, it became apparent that there had been no real reason for the long delay in the first place. Johnson gave the men a limited time to work out the details of completing and opening the bridge and the road, and then told them to report back—not with excuses, but with the job done.

I could tell by the surprised looks on their faces that taking direct action was a new experience for them, but they did it, and with Johnson's help and guidance it took a few weeks to accomplish something that would have taken months or years if each agency had sent out letters in stilted government legalese. The completion of this project meant a lot to people on both sides of the border.

Lyndon Johnson was also a "can do" president, as he proved in 1965 when the Highway Beautification Act was on the floor of the House of Representatives for a final vote. This bill was a favorite of Lady Bird's, who aspired to removing billboards from the horizon and ugly abandoned cars from highways. Johnson had sent invitations to most of the congressmen and their wives to attend a dinner and an evening of entertainment that was to take place on the night they were due to vote on the bill. It was to be a star-studded event, and the Johnson staff had been working on the arrangements for many weeks. Some of the brightest personalities of the New York stage, including members of the Metropolitan Opera, had signed on for the event. Johnson expected such a large turnout that the guests were scheduled to go from the White House to the State Department auditorium for the performance.

The "in Tuesday, out Thursday" set in the House of Representatives, the men who leave their wives at home and come to Washington only when there are midweek votes scheduled, had invited their wives to this party. Most of them came, wearing new dresses for the occasion, thrilled about going to the White House, where many of them had never been. They were looking forward to a gala evening, and to meeting and learning more about President Johnson. They learned plenty that night.

At about 5:30 that afternoon, President Johnson made the first of many phone calls to the House of Representatives. He told the congressmen that he expected them to pass "that bill of Lady Bird's" before they arrived at the White House that evening. The vote was going to be close, and Johnson's remarks were not universally appreciated in the House. Republicans tacked on numerous amendments and resorted to every delaying tactic they could think of. Congressman Jerry Ford of Michigan, minority leader of the House, was leading the Republicans that night.

Soon the galleries began to fill with wives dressed for dinner at the White House. From my seat in the gallery, I watched them motion to their husbands to meet them outside, but the husbands motioned right back at their wives to have patience, it would just take a little longer. Nearly all the members stayed on the floor.

The debate extended past the cocktail hour. Husbands

and wives began meeting in the House restaurant for a cup of coffee. The debate went on. Everyone began to get hungry. They could only think of the sumptuous feast Johnson had waiting in silver serving dishes on banquet tables at the White House. Long past the dinner hour, couples began eating in the House restaurant. All the steaks went early. Then there were sandwiches and, later, scrambled eggs. The restaurant finally announced they had no more bread.

It was a bad night for everyone, particularly for the entertainers who were waiting to perform. Finally, at 1:40 A.M., the beautification bill passed. By then, only a handful of the congressmen were energetic enough to go to the White House. Although I had an invitation, I went home to work on my story and to go to sleep. Representative Samuel Halpern of New York did go, though, and he told me how eerie it was to be one of the few people at the party in the great open spaces of the White House at that hour of the morning.

Another of Johnson's methods of getting the job done was described to me by Hobart Taylor, Jr., a black lawyer from Houston and Detroit who was the second generation of his family to work with Johnson. Hobart's father was eastern Texas's number one token black. For years, Hobart Senior was the only black man to represent Texas at national Democratic conventions. His son, who was Johnson's White House counsel, told me, "Every time I would bring him a paper, I knew that it would be shifted right back to me if I had not pursued all angles and all possible solutions." This was what Johnson expected in a staff report. He wanted his aides to "cover" the matter thoroughly before they brought it to him for consideration. I felt sorry for the man who had not done his work.

Along with his great drive for accomplishment, for getting things done, Johnson had a tremendous desire to be liked. This was caused in part by insecurity, but I like to think it was more than that. Johnson genuinely liked to give people pleasure.

And he loved pleasure himself. One of Lyndon Johnson's greatest private pleasures was flying over his ranch in a small plane in the late afternoon to look for deer. He invited me to ride along once. Of course I went—it was a wonderful chance to be with Lyndon and Lady Bird and hear him talk. We flew over his ranch and the neighboring ranches of the West family too. The deer came out in clusters. They were very small and not the same color as the ones I'd seen in Virginia. For once, LBJ seemed oblivious of politics, and spent the whole flight pointing out ranches and animals.

Johnson also loved riding on the vice-president's small yacht on the Potomac, and he loved driving, but only in Texas. Johnson never drove in the District of Columbia. He once told me, after I had an accident in my own car, that he thought it was too dangerous to drive in Washington, and that he felt it was better for him to use the time to concentrate on his work and not give any of his attention to driving. Therefore, one could often see him working or reading as his limousine, equipped with telephone and reading lamp, would go through Rock Creek Park with his faithful driver, Norman Edwards, at the wheel. Norman, who knew thousands of secrets, told me he would never write a book.

Lyndon loved to eat, too, and nothing tasted better to him than a snack of summer sausage and cheese picked up from a roadside German country store on the long ride from San Antonio to the ranch. He always laced these snacks with generous drinks of Cutty Sark from the small container kept for this purpose in the back of his car, easily accessible to Johnson and to his passengers. His secretary, Dorothy Nichols, drove the car. At times, Johnson's love of good living approached the bizarre. He and A. W. Moursand, a close friend, business partner, and lawyer who lived near Johnson's ranch, had a lookout tower built in the hill country from which they could shoot deer and wild turkey. I never saw Johnson shoot from the tower, but it was built for that purpose and completely equipped for a long wait. Approached by an elevator, it had a stove, a refrigerator, and a carpeted floor. Johnson liked to keep the tower secret, and when he once showed it to me proudly, he asked me to keep the shooting tower off the record.

Good living to LBJ also meant keeping several Lincoln Continentals and jeeps around the ranch, all of which were equipped with a private intercar communications system. He liked to keep up a running conversation with drivers and passengers in the cars that followed him in procession as he dashed around the countryside, driving anywhere from 90 to 100 miles per hour. There was practically no traffic, but one never knew when an absentee landlord would be visiting his country place and suddenly pop out of one of the side roads, or when a farmer would decide to drive to town. But Johnson never considered that other cars might be on the road when he drove. It was all the more dangerous because the rolling hills obscured the horizon. After he drove her around the ranch for the first time, Marianne Means told Johnson, "Mr. President, you're fun!"

Johnson's love of speed was a real problem for guests at the ranch. If they survived the drives with Johnson, they still had to face a ride in his boat. Johnson often raced his small cabin cruiser down the lake beside his other lakeside ranch. If a guest declined to go along, Johnson applied the pressure. He loved taking people out on that boat. But the guests who did go breathed a lot easier once they returned to land. Johnson drove his boat the way he drove his cars, and I've never been gladder to get off *anything*. I will say, though, that a ride on Johnson's boat made one of those expertly cooked steaks taste all the better when eaten after a couple of drinks on the firm ground of Johnson's patio.

I will never forget one particular drive with Johnson (who was then vice-president) and his entourage, speeding through the hill country. I must have been riding in the third car. To this day, I don't know how we didn't all end up in a telescopic crash, for as we came up fast over a hill, trying to keep up with LBJ, we suddenly saw that the cars in front were stopped dead in the road. Standing against the horizon with his arms held aloft of his six-foot-plus frame was Lyndon Johnson. He was holding a heavy rock in both hands and looking down at the ground at a giant rattle-snake.

He hit the snake with the rock, but the blow didn't kill it. Then he ordered Rufus Youngblood, his Secret Service bodyguard, to shoot the snake. But the persistent snake still would not die. Perhaps it was an old political enemy of Johnson's, reincarnated. As I recall, it took three shots from the White House super marksman to kill the snake. Everyone but me got back into the cars to continue our drive. But I would not leave the dead snake on the ground. Much to the amazement of my traveling companions, I asked that the snake be picked up and brought along. My companions, Bob Baskin of the *Dallas News* and Vernon Louviere of the *Houston Chronicle*, pointed out that it was a weekend, and that I could not possibly find a taxidermist. "I don't care," I said, "I am taking that snake home to hang on my wall. It isn't every Texas rattler that has been hit with a rock by the vice-president of the United States and shot three times by a Secret Service agent." We took the snake.

Later, the two newsmen arranged to have the snake put in my pathway near the patio where it would frighten me in the fading light. It was their fault, and Johnson's, that that snake never made it back to Washington with me. I finally put it on the outside of the car in which I was traveling, where I thought it would not offend the nostrils or the delicate sensibilities of the two men. But Johnson asked us if we minded changing cars, as he wanted to drive in our car with A. W. Moursand and talk business. I forgot all about my snake. En route back to the ranch, Johnson drove the car carrying my snake at ninety-five miles an hour, and Vernon, who was driving our car and who was unfamiliar with the roads, the controls, and the radio communications system, had trouble keeping up in the fast-growing darkness. Later, when we were back at the ranch, I thought of my snake and went to look for it on the side of Johnson's car. It was gone. I shook my finger in Johnson's face and said, "You drove ninety-five miles an hour—so fast that my snake fell off."

"No," he replied calmly, "I never drive that fast. You must be mistaken."

Lyndon and Lady Bird always tried to make me and their other guests comfortable and at home at their ranch. They took me right into their family circle. I felt a little awkward on my first visit, but not for long. When I found Lyndon having breakfast in bed (as I remember it, he was eating his favorite deer sausage, which combined venison and pork), he insisted that I come in, sit by the bed, and have my breakfast right there, too. I remember Lady Bird putting the food on her plate and climbing back in the bed beside him.

Johnson loved his ranch and was as demanding a boss in Texas as he was in Washington. I remember when his ranch hands told him that they couldn't figure out why the pavement on his landing strip kept breaking up. Very early one Sunday morning, I tiptoed downstairs to go to church and I came upon Lyndon in his pajamas, standing by the kitchen window and staring out at the landing strip. "I knew it," I heard him say, "the sheep walk across that runway every morning." Johnson's ranch hands told him the livestock never went near that part of the ranch.

Whether he was at the ranch or in Washington, Johnson was a great storyteller. The stories were especially good because they were usually true and always about people we knew. Some of his stories were elaborations on events many of the reporters were already familiar with. He repeated conversations that occurred when we were too far away to hear, or that took place after a press conference ended. He seemed to remember every detail. Johnson had a remarkable memory, and I believe he could remember everything anyone ever said to him.

One of Johnson's best stories described a dramatic moment in his own life. Johnson, newly arrived in Washington as a clerk to a congressman, was rooming with a fellow Texan, Arthur Perry, who worked for Texas Senator Tom Connally. They lived in a basement apartment at the old Dodge Hotel. Johnson was not used to the cold dampness of Washington, and he contracted pneumonia. He was seriously ill, and it looked as if he would not survive. A friend of Johnson's father, sensing the seriousness of the illness, came to sit by the young man's bedside. He listened to his labored breathing for many hours. Finally, perspiration appeared on the young man's brow. The crisis had passed. When Johnson opened his eyes, beside him was the man destined to be a father to him in politics and in public life from then on—Sam Rayburn, the man who served as Speaker of the House of Representatives longer than anyone in history.

Some of Johnson's best stories were told at parties. He and Lady Bird were great party givers. They were most generous with their hospitality, and their parties ranged from Tex-Mex suppers and informal barbeques to cocktail parties and elegant dinners. Johnson's stories always attracted a crowd at these parties. When Johnson was in the room, I never bothered much with anyone else. I remember being absolutely incensed with one of my escorts because he wanted to talk, not listen. When Johnson was around, everyone else did the listening—he did the talking.

At one party I remember, a lawn party in Chevy Chase, Maryland (a Washington suburb), hosted by a congressman's brother and his wife, Johnson was in the center of an attentive crowd as usual. It was nearly ten at night, and Johnson was really starting to warm up when he suddenly said, "Sarah, go get me a cup of Sanka." Just as I would have done in Texas had one of my older brothers so requested, I went into the house to oblige. Much to my horror, our hostess had no Sanka. I was surprised. I thought everyone knew that Johnson didn't drink coffee at night, only Sanka. Most people who were going to entertain Johnson were prepared, and many friends kept Sanka on their pantry shelf just in case he ever came by.

The hostess did not seem to be at all perturbed. She had no Sanka and that was that. She turned to other things.

I was troubled, though, because I knew that I'd get blamed; I would be the one to disappoint him. What really worried me was the possibility that he would get up and go home, and that we wouldn't hear any more of those wonderful stories. I couldn't let that happen. But what was I to do? It didn't take me long to make up my mind. I would find him some Sanka, even if I had to go to every house in Chevy Chase to do it. I went out from door to door until I found a neighbor who had what I was looking for. I brought the Sanka back, made him a cup, and never said where I got it. By the time I got back to the party, he was asking whatever happened to his Sanka. "Here it is," I replied, and the stories kept coming.

Airplane rides with Johnson were wonderful occasions to hear stories, too. There were usually five to ten reporters clustered around him on these trips. The narrow plane aisles made it hard to hear Johnson's low voice and, at times, we would climb over the backs of the seats, sit on armrests, or just stand as long as we could, trying not to miss one word. Johnson would pause now and then to ask for a refill of Cutty Sark, and kept munching all the time on nuts and snacks. This is probably why I never saw him get drunk. Now and then on these trips, when he had not eaten a real meal, I would try to get him to eat. "Not yet," he would say, or, "I'm not hungry now." On one flight, when it was past midnight and we had not yet eaten, I went back to the rear of the plane and told the steward that I would have my dinner. When I returned to my seat, Johnson wanted to know where I'd been. He was furious when I told him that I had eaten. Why hadn't I waited for him? Finally, at about 2:00 A.M., Johnson announced that he was ready to eat his dinner.

There was usually someone on the plane who could fix drinks for Johnson, but not always. Before he was vice-president, I traveled with LBJ on rented (and borrowed) planes when no stewards were available and when there was no cooked food on board. On flights like that, we all joined in and waited on ourselves. One of Johnson's secretaries was frequently called on to double as a stewardess. Once, Mrs. Johnson's niece, Diana MacArthur, went with us to help out. I got the distinct impression that some member of the family or of Johnson's staff usually went along on these trips to serve as a chaperone as well as to act as a stewardess. I believe Bill Moyers was originally hired because Lady Bird was disturbed about the gossip surrounding Johnson's frequent trips with female staff members.

In 1961 I was one of the lucky reporters who accompanied Vice-President Lyndon Johnson on a trip around the world. The Austin and Waco papers sent me and I also wrote for other papers during the trip. Johnson wanted to have Texas reporters along on this trip, not only for companionship, but so that we could report his exploits to the folks back home. Johnson's trip may have been more important, deliberate, and meaningful than the goodwill mission it appeared to be, but one incident in Southeast Asia convinced me that there had not been sufficient prior preparation for the trip, no matter what its purpose.

When the official party arrived in Taiwan, it was obvious to me that everything was not as it should have been. During our afternoon visit, Madame Chiang Kai-shek spent but a few crisply polite minutes with Lady Bird Johnson and did not offer to show her around, to guide her tour (as we had been told she would do), or to present the schoolchildren who were scheduled to sing. Madame said that she had to return to the palace to work, and her tone of voice made it clear that more important matters awaited her. I was shocked.

Later in the afternoon, I discovered that there were

doubts as to when, for how long, and even *if* the generalissimo would see the vice-president of the United States. It seemed that both Chiang and Madame (who ruled right along with him) believed that Johnson had come to lecture them, or to scold them, or to tell them the bad news about a forthcoming cut in United States aid. I certainly did not know whether or not such instructions had been given to the vice-president, but I didn't think so. The fact that the Chinese were so wary, though, indicated to me that the Johnsons' trip had not been properly planned. Every high official of government needs careful, well-thought-out advance work before he leaves home base on any mission, and the reason for his trip must not be misunderstood if he is to succeed.

I had looked forward to this visit because I felt it would be a chance for American reporters to learn more about Nationalist China and, in particular, about its leaders in order to determine whether their regime deserved our continued support. I knew that some of my colleagues on the trip looked down their noses at Taiwan before we arrived, and some had written off our trip as unimportant. I thought it was very important for the American people to learn more about our mysterious allies. Therefore I was extremely disappointed when I was informed that the generalissimo would not see the American press. The visit appeared to be a failure.

I gathered up all my courage and asked to see the top Chinese official in the information bureau, the man who had made the arrangements for our visit. Looking back, I honestly don't know how I got the nerve to speak up, but at the time it seemed to me as if I was the only one who could save our trip. I explained that a newspaper for which I worked, William Loeb's *Manchester Union-Leader*, supported the Free Chinese government and had in the past gone out on a fairly long limb to endorse its aims. The Chinese had heard of Loeb, and they were even more impressed when I mentioned the name of Senator Styles Bridges of New Hampshire, a powerful Republican who had great influence with Democrats as well as with his own party. I told the Chinese that Bridges was their friend, that I covered him daily in Washington, and that the senator who fought Free China's battles in Congress would be very disappointed if he heard from me when I returned to America that their leader had refused to meet with us. I also tried to convey the importance of sending a message back to the citizens of the United States. I finished by telling the information officer that I was a good friend of both Styles Bridges and Lyndon Johnson.

Our meeting had taken place late in the day. I turned away from the information officer sadly, disappointed that there would be no story. I was terribly let down, and to make things worse, I had to share a room with CBS's Nancy Dickerson again. Every stop we made on the trip, when we arrived at the next hotel, I'd run to the front desk to try to get a room of my own and so would she. Neither of us liked this arrangement, but we were constantly being put together, and most of our rooms were small, crowded, and unattractive. Besides the fact that Nancy and I got in each other's way, our work schedules frequently conflicted. Nancy was a perfectionist. Since she was a broadcast journalist, she would practice by dictating her stories into a tape recorder over and over. She also played back the tapes a lot. I, of course, typed my stories, frequently late at night when Nancy was trying to sleep.

But later, after I got back to the Dickerson-McClendon room, I found that everything had changed. The Chinese didn't know whether or not President Kennedy had sent Johnson to give them some bad news, but they did know who Styles Bridges was. The Chinese came to us that evening to say that Vice-President and Mrs. Johnson had been invited to see Chiang and Madame at their country house the next day, and that the press would follow in our own bus. I was promised personally that there would be a question-and-answer session with the generalissimo.

When we arrived and saw the two leaders together, I knew instantly that there had been a change in their relationship. They were smiling, and Madame was cordiality itself. I don't know if Lyndon Johnson ever knew how close he came to failure on our trip to Taiwan, because I never told him what I did. But I could see that he was bursting out all over with pride and pleasure that afternoon, and that the meeting was a success. Outside on the lawn, the American reporters had their picture taken with both men and their wives as if we were one big happy family.

Maybe Johnson did know something, though. Just before the picture was taken, he called for me to come stand up in front.

I still have that picture.

# 7

## The Democrats' Watergate

Lyndon Johnson's behavior at a press conference was very similar to his behavior at a party. He grabbed the spotlight and never gave it up. His concept of a press conference was totally different from mine. To Johnson, a press conference was (or should be) an occasion to announce a new plan or policy, a chance to present a carefully prepared statement and image to the press. Like Eisenhower, Johnson hated the give-and-take of press conferences, and had hated them since he was a member of the House of Representatives. Johnson always wanted to do all the talking, and even as a congressman he resented reporters who asked questions. And if a reporter interrupted his train of thought by asking a question on a subject other than the one Johnson was discussing, that reporter was sure to feel the Johnson wrath.

I will never forget how astonished I was when Johnson cut off my questions during one of the one-sided press conferences he held when he was in the Senate. He talked for thirty straight minutes, exhausting us all, and then tried to leave without taking one question. He was furious when I challenged him as he tried to walk out. He wouldn't answer me, though; he just glared at me and left.

Johnson behaved the same way wherever he was. I remember the first time he invited me to have lunch with him and Lady Bird at the Capitol. I looked forward to it for days, and spent hours preparing myself to be an interesting conversationalist. But when we were seated at the table, and when I tried to get a word in, failed, and then tried and failed again, I realized that no one else was expected to talk—just the great man himself. So I sat back, relaxed, and listened. That was the beginning of many a long listen—but Lyndon Johnson usually had something colorful to talk about.

Lyndon Johnson's stories were usually about events and people of the current scene. Many had to do with what he had said or done for people because Johnson loved to make others happy. He had a great sense of what was fitting and dramatic.

Take the time he decided, when Germany's Chancellor Konrad Adenauer died in 1967, that the Bavarian priest from the little picture-postcard church near the Johnson ranch at Stonewall, Texas, should be flown to the funeral as a guest. No one was more surprised than Father Schneider, but Johnson thought he should go to the funeral because he had said Mass for Adenauer at St. Xavier's church when the chancellor had visited Johnson at his Texas ranch and the large community of descendants of German refugees of the mid-eighteenth century who now live near Fredericksburg, Texas.

As Johnson told the story afterward, he had given strict instructions that when Father Schneider's plane arrived in Germany, the president of the United States, who had preceded him, was to be awakened. It was 3:00 A.M. when the plane reached Germany. Per instructions, the president received Father Schneider in his hotel suite. Would he have some tea? The priest could not quite understand it all. Here was the president of the United States offering him—as Johnson described it—"a ticket" for the front row of the funeral Mass in the cathedral at Cologne. At the ceremonies, Prime Minister Harold Wilson of Great Britain was most curious about "this famous priest."

Johnson did not hesitate to talk to reporters about other reporters. He confided to Norma Milligan of *Newsweek*, to whom he liked to talk for long periods, that he had been reading repeatedly in the *New York Times* in a column by Scotty Reston about this or that matter being "on Johnson's mind."

"How can he know what's on my mind when he has not been to see me?" asked Johnson. When he inquired of his staff and the press office whether Reston had been visiting with them, none admitted having seen or talked with Reston.

A year later, Johnson told reporters, "James Reston came to see me this week. I took him over to the mansion for lunch. Guess what he wrote about me later? 'Lyndon Johnson feels sorry for himself.' "

One of my favorite stories about Johnson is what he said to me one morning at the Capitol. At the time, the President's Cup Regatta was going to be held on the Potomac and his daughter, Lynda Bird, had been named queen. She could have two attendants, so she had chosen a friend from Texas and my daughter, Sally O'Brien. "Hey," said the vice-president, "I just learned—the reason Lynda asked Sally to be her attendant is not because you're a newspaperwoman but because she likes Sally."

"I knew that," I replied.

Before Johnson left the White House he tried to take care of friends in government and to place them in key places where they might be of future help to him or his party. Two military aides, James Cross, an air force pilot, and Colonel Jack Albright, were going to be made generals. But before they could become generals, they had to go to command and general staff school. This meant they had to leave the White House. Apparently forgetting about this, Johnson woke early one day and called for his military aides. Cross was not there. Albright was not there. Johnson was in his flowing robe and well lathered when a new military aide, Haywood Smith of the Marine Corps, who had been hastily summoned by the telephone operator, entered his room.

"Good morning, Mr. President," sang out Smith cheerily. "What can I do for you?"

Johnson walked straight to him, moving in so close the lather almost brushed Smith's face, and boomed, "Haywood, I'm not ever going to make you a general. Do you understand?" By this time, Smith was paler than a marine gets in battle. He wondered what he had done to deserve this rebuke. "Here I make Cross a general and Albright a general, and I can't find either of them when I need them," said Johnson.

Johnson found out early in life that it could be very helpful to develop a father-son relationship with older newspaper editors. He did them favors, gave them stories, became their friend. Harry Provence, who worked for the *Waco News-Tribune*, which was part of the Marsh-Fentress chain in Texas, was such an avid fan of Johnson's that he would have done anything editorially possible to please him. The whole chain of Marsh-Fentress papers was so obviously behind Johnson that LBJ might have been Fentress's own son. The word was out to Marsh-Fentress reporters and editors to protect Johnson by writing and publishing only what he wanted the public to read about himself. Both Johnson and Harlon Fentress, the top owner-editor, told me this.

Johnson wanted to control the news totally, and his attempts to do so were outrageous, but typical and usually effective. Besides Provence, Johnson had Houston Harte in his corner. Harte, the editor of the *San Angelo Standard-Times*, used to examine advance copy of Drew Pearson's column for possible criticism of LBJ. If Drew said anything Lyndon might not like, Harte would get right on the phone to Johnson, who then called the editor of every newspaper in Texas that carried the column. He asked each one not to print it that day and, surprisingly, they often did what he asked.

When I wrote the very first story exposing Bobby Baker's illegal business dealings, Harry Provence, then my editor, called Johnson. Baker was then secretary to the Senate majority party (the Democrats), and I referred to him in my article as Johnson's "protégé." After all, Johnson had been Baker's boss when he was Senate majority leader, and the two went back a long way together. But Johnson, who was vice-president when I wrote the story, wanted to put as much distance as possible between himself and Baker, the glorified Senate page who was beginning to have the smell of scandal around him.

Like most reporters, I knew Bobby Baker as a friendly, extremely helpful source for stories in the Senate. But I had read a newspaper story that made me wonder about him. The story described Baker boasting to a group of political interns who were touring the Capitol that he held the votes of ten senators in the palm of his hand. James McCartney, who wrote the story for the *Chicago Daily News*, told me that when he checked the story with Baker the secretary to the Senate majority didn't deny it but indicated, with his gestures and facial expressions, that he did control those senators and that, furthermore, he liked having the truth known.

So I was already interested in Baker when I noticed a small item in the *Washington Post* saying that Baker was being sued in civil court by someone named Ralph Hill. I didn't know Hill, but I went to see him to check out the story. "Where are the other reporters?" Hill asked when I arrived at his office. I was the only reporter there. Hill, who ran a vending machine company, told me that Baker had obtained a lucrative contract for Hill's firm with a large defense subcontractor near Washington. I had often heard stories around Capitol Hill that Bobby Baker could accurately predict, to a privileged few, which company would be awarded the next government defense contract.

The Bobby Baker case far outweighs the Watergate case from the standpoint of outright corruption in government, in the obstruction of justice by a president in the White House and by sitting members of the Senate, as well as officials in the Justice Department, and in the number of lives of people touched. In fact, this case is bigger than the Teapot Dome scandal, I wrote my editors shortly after the story broke. To this day, I believe I was right.

Of course, in the Baker case, all was not allowed to come out. Had it not been for the massive dirty tricks done by the White House and the Senate committee, the Baker story might have been allowed to develop in areas that were never touched or, at the most, skimmed over. Had it not been for the persuasiveness of a sitting president—Lyndon B. Johnson—the cooperation of a J. Edgar Hoover and his FBI, the determination of senators to stranglehold the Senate Rules Committee's hearings on Baker, I believe the nation might have seen the resignation of a president or his impeachment before Watergate.

As it was, the dirty tricks led to changes in the sitting members of the United States Supreme Court and to a shift in attorneys general. That Court saw for the first time a solicitor general of the United States confessing in public that the Justice Department had been guilty of wiretapping. While all this puppetry was being played by President Johnson and his clever adviser, Abe Fortas, the public never guessed that it was being done to keep hidden the truth about the operations of Baker and his cohort, Fred Black of Joplin, Missouri, a Washington consultant for North American Aviation Corporation. The real purpose was to keep Black from talking about what had gone on in the Senate, activities which allegedly involved others than Black and Baker.

In some ways, if the Baker case had been fully pursued, it could have been a warning to the other political party, some surmise today. Thus, they theorize, Watergate might never have happened. Whether this is true or not, one cannot say for sure. The fact that the Baker affair was exposed is cause for a deep sense of national gratitude to the two individuals who made this possible. One was Ralph Hill, who filed a civil court suit against Baker, setting forth various Baker activities in connection with a vending machine contract in defense plants. The other was Senator John Williams, a Republican from Delaware who, after he saw the suit, learned of Baker's extracurricular activities in and about the Senate in connection with a myriad of money-making enterprises. He then demanded that Senate Democrats get rid of Baker. Baker at the time was actually an employee of the whole Senate, so Williams had a right to do this.

Many others around the Senate had long suspected that there was something wrong going on in the Baker suite of offices, but they had not been able to get at the facts until Hill filed suit. One of these was Mrs. Grace E. Johnson, who for thirteen years was a Senate professional staff member.

As soon as the Hill suit was filed, I figured this was a chance to get something on the record so that I would at last be able to write a story about the goings-on in Baker's office.

Senator Williams checked on the case. What he found led him straight to the office of Senate Majority Leader Mike Mansfield of Montana, who had earlier discounted what was happening. In fact, Mansfield had given an interview saying that Baker would stay. But after he talked with Williams he knew that Baker had to go. Therefore Mansfield issued a statement saying he regretted "the necessity" for accepting Baker's resignation.

Mansfield's action followed a meeting he called in his office. Baker did not attend. His friends Senator Hubert Humphrey of Minnesota and Senator George Smathers of Florida were there. When they heard what Williams knew, they realized the jig was up for Baker.

Then Williams put through a resolution in the Senate, authorizing an investigation of Baker's activities and providing for some permanent reform to make sure that Senate employees did not follow Baker's example in the future.

Thus was provided the machinery for the Senate Rules Committee hearings. Williams was backed by Senator John Sherman Cooper of Kentucky, who urged that the Senate employ an outside attorney fully capable of handling the investigation. Williams and Cooper were aided, as the hearings proceeded, by Senators Clifford Case of New

Jersey, Carl Curtis of Nebraska, and occasionally by Hugh Scott of Pennsylvania, although at times it appeared that Scott might be helping Baker. Once Scott went to a dinner at the White House and returned saying he was sure that President Johnson had no ties to the Baker business dealings in the Senate.

Also determined that his friend Baker not be given a rough time was the oldest man in the Senate, Senator Carl Hayden of Tempe, Arizona, a power despite the fact that he was nearing ninety years of age. Senator Howard Cannon, a Democrat from Nevada, had some relationship with Baker dealings, as did Smathers. Senator Robert Byrd of West Virginia had worked closely with Baker during the Kennedy-Humphrey rivalry in the West Virginia presidential primary on the Humphrey side. He appeared to be a friendly advocate of Baker during the time when the Lyndon Johnson faction, seeking an opportunity to knock out Kennedy's candidacy early in hopes of helping Johnson get the nomination, was secretly providing money, campaign literature, and manpower to aid Humphrey. Baker was the emissary between the Johnson forces and the Humphrey organization in West Virginia. In fact, Baker's Senate office was the site of a secret cache of Humphrey campaign literature.

With this as a background, the hearings got off to a shaky start, and although a professional was employed, there was unenthusiastic cooperation with the Baker prosecution on the part of Senate committee staff members and former FBI agents who were assigned to the case. The upshot was that there were gaps in subject matter covered, in requirements for witnesses to appear and tell all, and finally there was a committee denunciation of a key anti-Baker witness, Don Reynolds.

As soon as Hill filed the case, seeking $300,000 damages from Baker, Senate pages who operated under Baker spread the word that Hill was mentally ill. Later, Baker started the rumor that Hill had been in a hospital during his service in the air force. Actually, Hill had a busy combat record and after the war served some time in the active reserve unit in Washington. He produced papers to prove he had not been hospitalized.

As the word got around that there was to be trouble for Baker, Humphrey lost no time in telephoning then Vice-President Lyndon B. Johnson in Iceland, urging him to cut short a European trip and come home at once.

When Johnson arrived, he immediately used a cooling and shushing process on the wire services at the Senate. He did this most effectively.

Baker summoned Robert Albright of the *Post* and some other reporters to his office to say he was innocent and would sue for libel anyone printing anything about Hill's accusations. That was before Baker resigned.

All this had the desired effect of hushing up the story, with one exception. The only problem with the media that Johnson encountered was my story.

I obtained the first story on the Baker case in print outside of Washington and the first story that told of the Baker financial empire operating from the United States Capitol. This was carried on the North American Newspaper Alliance wire, now owned and operated by United Features syndicate.

The NANA syndicate stood for many years (and still remains) as a unique factor in journalism in the United States because it was the only service that used stories from Washington reporters as well as staff-originated material. Thus there were times when the only means of getting out stories nationally from Washington on a subject was through NANA. Otherwise, some stories would have remained bottled up from the public.

Sometime later, Sid Goldberg, NANA's editor, wrote the secretary of the Standing Committee of Correspondents of the Senate Press Gallery as follows:

> North American Newspaper Alliance is nominating Sarah McClendon for the Raymond Clapper Award for her consistently good coverage of the Bobby Baker scandal. It was Miss McClendon, through her story for N.A.N.A. in September, 1963, who first broke this story in its full ramifications on a national basis, as she explains in her enclosed letter. She followed this throughout 1964 with exclusives on Baker that add up to an impressive display of enterprising reporting.

Who was this man, Bobby Baker, and what had he done that was so incredible?

Bobby Baker's story is important to all students of government because it teaches how power can be acquired over a legislative branch of a powerful government by persons who may not be widely known for leadership, talents, or skill—in short, nobodies. They can obtain power behind the scenes. This can be done by using the bureaucracy that exists even in the legislative branch. A power within government can gain control over people in government or the citizens in general before they know it exists. It is quite probable that Baker would have operated indefinitely with growing powers had it not been for the fact that the existence of his kingdom was exposed on a court record and then by a follow-up by the press. In this case, exposure came, oh, so slowly—quite in contrast with the Watergate capture.

There may be other Bobby Bakers lurking inside other smaller bureaucracies without disclosures.

Baker was a skinny youth of fourteen who came to Washington from Pickens, South Carolina, when South Carolina Senators Burnet Maybank and Olin Johnston appointed him a page. In eight years, he had become a leader of other pages. He had ingratiated himself with leading senators who came to like him. He became secretary to the Senate majority, the Democrats. He was patronizing to another young South Carolinian, Ralph Hill, of Green Sea, whose first job in Washington was in the Senate library. Hill went into private business. Baker stayed at the Senate. Hill found that to make a living in Washington, one did better if one knew certain people on the hill, as Congress is called.

Bobby Baker built his private business empire right in the Senate. It covered real estate in Puerto Rico, meat in Haiti, the Dominican Republic, Hawaii, Las Vegas, and property in Florida; stock purchases in Michigan; a Howard Johnson restaurant in North Carolina; a California bank; interests in the aerospace industry in California and the aircraft business in Texas; Serv-U Corporation, a vending machine company that served defense plants nationwide; commissions from a meat-importing company using Caribbean stockyards; stock in an Oklahoma City bank; and ownership of a plush resort hotel called the Carousel at North Ocean City, Maryland, catering to Washington officialdom.

Wasn't it odd that the senators never noticed his increased holdings? Perhaps the only one who knew how extensive Baker's business dealings were was the late Senator Robert Kerr of Oklahoma. It was not that Baker served him; rather, through loans of money, Kerr bought

Bobby and all that went with him, including his ability to count votes in the Senate for health legislation in favor of Kerr at a vital time. (Baker had been cut into a bank stock ownership by Kerr.) The Kennedys, who were striving valiantly to pass this legislation for the country, thus suffered a defeat on the one occasion when they trusted Baker, even though they had felt all the time that they should not depend on him. They accepted Baker's judgment as to the appropriate time to take the vote in the Senate—and suffered a critical defeat. Baker had counted the votes and had told the Kennedys they would win. In the end, the vote came out in favor of Kerr, who was leading the opposition to the health bill.

Baker bought stock for around $27,000 in a firm called Mortgage Guarantee Insurance Corporation, also called MAGIC, two days before it was listed with the Securities and Exchange Commission. Did Baker know it would be listed? I don't know. But his stock went up so high he chalked up a profit of some $70,000. Baker then used this as security to get other loans.

Baker had a partnership with Don Reynolds of Silver Spring, who was in the insurance business. Baker also had a law practice downtown in Washington with Ernest Tucker, whose name showed up as straw man or officer of companies in which Baker was interested. In a dispute that arose, Tucker sided with Baker against Tucker's wife, who worked for Bobby as his confidential secretary. But suddenly Bobby seemed to have some secrets in an office safe that he did not want Margaret Tucker to know anything about. Baker fired her.

In the hearings later, she often could not remember much. She revealed nothing significant about Baker's dealings.

About this time there were displays of $100 bills on desks in Bobby's Capitol office. He loved to play with the money, to finger it.

No senators seemed to wonder where Baker got the money to buy the Carousel Hotel in Ocean City, Maryland. None seemed surprised or raised an inquiry when Baker's assistant, Walter Joe Stewart, was found using a Senate car to drive to the hotel in Ocean City. (In 1977 Stewart was back on the Senate floor counting votes, courtesy of Senate Majority Leader Robert Byrd, Democrat of West Virginia.)

The senators had in fact been props for the staging of a lavish coming-out party for the Carousel Hotel. Bobby chartered a bus to take many of them to Ocean City for the event. Vice-President Johnson and his wife, Lady Bird, attended, as did the late, famed Washington hostess, Perle Mesta, and Chief Robert Murray of the Washington Metropolitan Police Department.

The Carousel drew attention to Baker. While it did not bring about his downfall, it contributed to later events that played a major role in his questionable financial manipulations.

Don Reynolds was told by Tucker he would "hang" for telling the Senate about his experiences with Baker. Among other things, Reynolds told the Senate in executive session of large sums of money that came into Baker's hands from big corporations doing business with the government. He told senators that it was Baker to whom he referred a young woman who was pregnant and wanted an abortion. He talked it over with Bobby, who gave him a certain Capitol Hill telephone number for calling. She later telephoned Reynolds to "thank" him.

Abortions sometimes followed rendezvous between big

donors to the Democratic party and certain beautiful young girls who worked at the Capitol.

Baker would often recruit the young lovelies by saying, "Who wants to give out programs at the Democratic fund raising dinner?" They all wanted to make ten dollars and put on a pretty long dress and get into the evening's glamorous function. "Now, girls, I want you to work here until eleven o'clock," Baker would tell them, "and then you are on your own. Now, remember, be nice to our friends from out of town."

Sometimes the abortion mill on Capitol Hill (which the Senate Rules Committee later declined to investigate when looking into the Baker arena) operated through arrangements made at a downtown Washington restaurant. Sometimes it involved trips to Puerto Rico. There was a one-armed man who figured in some of the business dealings. A limousine would at times contact the parties in front of the Mayflower Hotel on Connecticut Avenue to carry them to a large country estate in southern Maryland. Usually those involved would surrender an envelope containing $2,500. The young women were allowed to keep $500 for having the abortions, which were sometimes performed at the manorlike estate frequented by a late wealthy Alabama congressman.

A number of senators had to know that Baker's secretary, Carole Tyler, ran a date bureau from her desk in Baker's office, for some of them were the partners in this social arrangement. Mainly, dates were obtained with the girls on Capitol Hill for wealthy financiers from out of town who liked to party in Washington. Carole often arranged the parties planned by Baker and paid for by the Murchison brothers of Dallas when they came to the nation's capital to further their long-range construction, oil, cattle, publishing, or other interests. Their business often depended on obtaining another government contract or passage of new legislation. They had a Washington lawyer, Thomas Webb, a former FBI man, but worked all their deals closely with Baker. Parties for senators were a regular part of their operations. They paid close attention to Lyndon Johnson and to another old friend, Senator Clint Anderson of New Mexico. But Anderson would tolerate none of Baker's secret dealings.

At one of these parties, Walter Jenkins, assistant to Vice-President Johnson, declined to stay. When the Murchison hosts asked why, Baker replied, "Oh, he likes boys." This was years before Jenkins had to resign from his post as assistant to President Lyndon Johnson at the White House, following an arrest for an alleged homosexual act in the men's room of the YMCA.

It was at the Baker parties where the beauty from East Germany, Ellen Rometsch, was introduced as a new find. Through Baker, she met Attorney General Robert Kennedy, General "Rosie" O'Donnell, and many senators and influential lobbyists. One investigator on a crucial Senate committee that was privy to many secrets wanted to give up his family to marry her.

Ellen Rometsch appeared on the Washington scene very suddenly. When she became too "hot" a package, she was just as swiftly deported by the Justice Department and Immigration Service under Bobby Kennedy.

Rometsch reportedly had not been married long when she came here as the wife of a German army sergeant. They had met at a bar. He worked for a German government office in the supply field. His agency on Wisconsin Avenue in Washington, D.C., was so secret that the U.S. State Department and German diplomats did not know of its existence. For some reason, the sergeant and his beautiful wife lived in a house far too expensive for a sergeant's salary in an affluent neighborhood in North Arlington. She started going to diplomatic and official parties at once. He worked. Ellen asked questions of military friends. It did not take her long to find out where interesting people went to parties. She began appearing on the diplomatic party circuit without her husband, either with men friends or other women. Then she met Baker. She would take a cab from Arlington to Baker's Quorum Club for lobbyists and congressional staffers across the street from the Senate office buildings. From there she progressed to the parties in downtown hotels, which the Murchisons paid for and Baker arranged.

Later, theorists toyed with the idea that Ellen was some sort of spy. If so, she was well placed to get information from top officials.

After she was deported, Clark Mollenhoff of the *Des Moines Register and Tribune* wrote a story saying her acquaintanceships reached into the White House itself.

At once, Attorney General Robert Kennedy pounced on him, despite their long, previously close friendship. Kennedy telephoned Mollenhoff and asked that he be at the Justice Department the next morning, a Sunday, to answer questions about how he obtained his information for that story.

The usually resourceful Mollenhoff was shattered. He telephoned a friend at 2:00 A.M. to discuss what he was going to say. He was extremely nervous.

The next day, with fear, Mollenhoff walked into the lion's den. No peaceful Sunday with family for him. He spent a long time there. Mollenhoff emerged to tell friends that he had not divulged any of his sources of news, despite pressures. He also picked up an item or two that he put into another story.

After Rometsch was sent home to Germany, reporters tried to contact her there but found she was completely inaccessible, guarded by men and fierce dogs and allowed no visitors. It was reported that her parents were under some surveillance. She allegedly had been born in East Germany. She was treated badly. No one ever seemed to know what happened to her. Dr. Joe Bailey of Washington recalls her great beauty with nostalgia. "She was far more beautiful than Elizabeth Ray, Wayne Hays's girlfriend," he told me.

Undaunted by any of this, Bobby was actually merrily continuing in a profitable, friendly sort of way.

He opened a bank in Washington, the first person in twenty-nine years to get a national charter in the District of Columbia. A friend of Baker's, Senator John Sparkman of the Senate Banking and Currency Committee, which had jurisdiction over confirmation of officials who give out bank charters, was allowed to buy stock in it, as were several other Alabama congressmen.

Baker had several Florida real estate ventures with Senator George Smathers of Florida. They were often seen talking in Senate hideaways and were very closemouthed about their business. (The Baker-Smathers relationships were never included in the Senate Rules Committee's public inquiry. It was believed their relations also included operations in the sugar industry in the West Indies. Smathers elected to bow out of his Senate seat. This was the same Smathers who was a close friend of both Presidents Kennedy and Nixon and the one who was involved with Nixon in Florida real estate. He located his office close to the White House under Nixon and remained ready for consultations.)

At a National Press Club dinner with LBJ, Senator Everett Dirksen and one of my favorites, House Speaker Sam Rayburn (right).

Saying hello to Jerry Ford was like shaking hands with an old neighbor.

President Kennedy didn't always like my press conference questions, but mostly we got along fine.

It's the old McClendon homestead in Tyler, Texas, where I grew up.

Early childhood pictures aren't always flattering, but I like this one.

Helping the Red Cross in my small way during World War I.

Growing up in Tyler with the hair styles of 1926.

Mother and I on the day I graduated from high school.

Here I'm Touchstone in a Tyler Junior College production of *As you like it*.

My family, left to right: my father Sidney, my sister Patience, mother, me, Annie, Martha, and Frank.

Baker, in cahoots with a large sugar industry tycoon in New York, once arranged for Vice-President Lyndon Johnson and Lady Bird to be official guests at the Juan Bosch inauguration in the Dominican Republic.

This was quite unusual. Any travel, especially from one country to another on the part of a vice-president, is initiated by the host country and arranged through the protocol office at the State Department with presidential approval. Sometime later, I learned that Baker had put together the whole package of this trip and that the State Department participation merely consisted in giving formal approval.

Baker's manipulations in the Dominican Republic and Puerto Rico were never fully explored by the Senate committee, but Walter Joe Stewart, Baker's assistant, and Carole Tyler, his secretary, were seen going many times to the islands on weekends.

Edward Levinson, a major gambling figure in Las Vegas and on the islands of the Caribbean, joined with Baker in Serv-U Corporation to place their vending machines in national defense plants. Levinson and Baker also showed up on rolls as stockholders in Senator Kerr's bank in Oklahoma City.

Baker probably tried to make people think that he and Kerr were partners. But when Kerr died, Baker was amazed to hear that he had not left a will. Kerr had made some of his arrangements for gifts ahead of time. Associates of Baker were horrified to hear him say, "Kerr did not leave a will!" Then, "Let's write him one."

Baker became one of Kerr's useful tools when Johnson sent him to Kerr. Baker was seeking a large sum to go into business. Lyndon did not have it to lend or did not want to lend it, so he suggested that Baker go to Kerr.

Just where Kerr's plans for Baker might have led, no

one can tell, because Kerr was as ambitious (and wealthy) a man as ever walked on the Senate floor. In fact, he actually talked over plans for a complete takeover of the Senate during a session with other senators at Senator Dennis Chavez's funeral in New Mexico. The colleagues came back horrified.

While knowing senators looked conveniently the other way, Baker went into the business of lobbying them for their votes to help the savings and loan industry. They knew for what purpose they were being invited by Baker to a plush party in the old Supreme Court room, that shrine of justice at the Capitol. They must have known that Glen Troop and other savings and loan lobbyists camped out in Baker's office.

Baker showed an interest in legislation to help the Freight Forwarders, a sort of orphan of the shipping industry. For this service, Myron Weiner, a lobbyist of the Forwarders, later told the Senate Rules Committee he paid Baker $5,000.

Baker was also a stockholder (with Robert P. Thompson, a Washington representative of the Murchisons) of the Tecon Corporation, the big construction firm owned by the Murchisons that was awarded huge government contracts.

Whereas Sherman Adams under Eisenhower admittedly made a few calls on behalf of New England textile manufacturer Bernard Goldfine, that was nothing compared to what Baker did for his friends or clients. He telephoned frequently to officials in the Justice, Agriculture, Defense, and Treasury Departments; the Small Business Administration; the Internal Revenue Service; the Federal Bureau of Investigation; and the Federal Housing Administration.

In fact, officials of MAGIC sought help from Baker about that company taking over all guaranteed loan business of the federal government. Baker was trying to help them. They wanted to get the business that was then being carried on by the Veterans Administration on housing and small businesses and farms for returning veterans and the business done by the Federal Housing Administration. Baker was the contact man for them to bring this about. They proposed to say that it was not right for the federal government to be in this business, but that it should be handled by private enterprise. They were to be the private enterprise. While this plan was widely discussed with some of the top officials in government, it never got anywhere, perhaps because Baker was relieved of his Senate job about that time.

A common thread in the Baker story was sex. There was always a lot of it wherever Baker operated. Sex was a business commodity as well as a hobby: He was attractive to women. Three women devoted to him, yet knowing his failings, usually lunched together daily at the Capitol: his wife, Dottie, who was in charge of the files at the supersecret Senate Internal Security Subcommittee and who earned an annual salary of $11,000; his secretary, Margaret Tucker, then wife of his downtown law partner, Ernest Tucker; and Trudie Novack, wife of his partner in the Carousel Hotel and a secretary on the staff of the Senate Small Business Committee.

They stayed loyal to Baker despite the sudden death of Trudie Novack's husband after an argument with Baker over the Carousel, Margaret Tucker's sudden discharge by Baker and her subsequent divorce from Ernest, and Dottie's having to put up with Bobby's girlfriend, Carole Tyler.

It was brought out in testimony that Baker had at times paid half of Carole's rent on an apartment at a plush suburban establishment in North Arlington. Later, he arranged through the use of his name for a government loan to enable her to get a town house in Southwest Washington, which she shared with girlfriends. At times, Carole had to provide in her home a room for the use of a Baker friend and his girl.

After Carole died in the ocean crash of a small airplane in which she and a pilot were taking an alleged joyride, Dottie accompanied Bobby to the funeral.

Years later, after he came home from prison where he served time for some of his alleged financial manipulations, Dottie finally left him and her Senate job on order of her doctor and moved to the West Coast.

Trudie, still at the Senate in 1975, both made and lost money as a result of the Baker partnership. Perhaps she could look back at Baker from a more coolly objective viewpoint than the others.

Her husband's death was found listed twice on records in Montgomery County, once as a suicide and once as a natural death. Trudie did not know this until I told her about it years later.

She had never quite understood what happened from the time she and her husband came downstairs to their garage one Saturday morning to go shopping. In the few minutes she left him to attend a washing machine, he suffered a blow on the head and was found dying beside his car. There was a hose nearby.

Baker, who was in the neighborhood, arrived soon afterward and asked to be left in charge of arrangements. Novack was taken to Dr. Joe Bailey, a friend and associate of both Baker and Novack. Baker talked to the police, who, after that, became secretive and at time denied reporters access to records.

Baker often worked through women contacts, in committees on the hill and in federal offices. He was often aware ahead of time when contracts would be let by the air force. His special knowledge at times had to come from inside the Pentagon, presumably right from the contracting office. Baker knew fully two months ahead of time that General Dynamics in Fort Worth was going to get the contract to build a new swing-wing plane, the TFX, now called the F-111. The final decision was reportedly made not by defense officials. They made the recommendation to the White House, where President Kennedy, somewhat influenced by Vice-President Johnson, decided the matter. Observers said the decision was based more on political reasons than military considerations. That, of course, was a matter of judgment. But Bobby Baker knew enough to tell Ralph Hill two months earlier that his vending machine business in Fort Worth would be highly profitable.

The amazing thing was that senators who had voted unanimously to hire Baker as their majority secretary seemed utterly stupid or purposely unaware of his far-flung business empire, which had developed under their noses. Then, after this was revealed, many of them participated in the big cover-up.

Hill thinks that if government employees had not been allowed to get by with this, as Baker did because of a weak investigation, there might never have been a similar attempt to grab power and cover up wrongdoing in the Watergate affair.

The first big attempt at a cover-up came when Vice-President Johnson rushed home from Iceland several days after the Hill case was filed in court. Johnson came back earlier than scheduled. At first, Johnson managed to get the wire services (and a few who made inquiries) to accept the concept that this was just a case of two competing business-men fighting over a contract.

But when he found out that I had written a news story

about Baker's outside business career and that I was
calling him "Vice-President Johnson's protégé," Johnson
decided that he had to silence me.

At 5:20 P.M. on Monday (after I had worked all weekend writing my story on Baker and then seeking an outlet
for it nationally), I received a telephone call at home from
Walter Jenkins. He requested that I return to the Capitol
at once. He wished to talk to me. His voice told me this
was important. He did not say what it was about. But
Johnson and I had long had an agreement that if he could
not see me and I wished information, I was to contact
Walter, who would either give it to me himself or find
Johnson. So I realized that this was no small matter.
Grudgingly, I went seven miles back to the Capitol at
day's end.

When I arrived, Walter said, "Sarah, we know that you
have been trying to peddle around the press gallery a story
about Baker in which you refer to him as the 'Vice-
President's protégé.' "

He went on to say that I need not deny it because he had
in his hand a copy of the story I had earlier sent to Texas.
It had been sent back to Johnson by one of my editors,
whose chief mandate from the Fentress family publications
had been to keep Lyndon Johnson happy and satisfied at
all times and to keep getting him elected, as Lyndon had
told me.

Walter explained that it was erroneous to call Baker a
"protégé" of the vice-president. After all, he said, Baker
worked for the Senate, not Johnson. Johnson had not
brought Baker to Washington, but South Carolina Senators Burnet Maybank and Olin Johnston had done so years
ago. In fact, Jenkins said, "Mr. Johnson has seen very little
of Baker since he became vice-president—hardly ever at
all."

I knew why that was. The Kennedys hated Baker and would not let him come to the White House. They knew of Baker's part in trying to defeat John F. Kennedy during the presidential campaign in West Virginia. They knew some (but not all) of the Baker tricks in Los Angeles on behalf of Johnson's candidacy for president. They also had other suspicions about Baker, so much so that they had ordered files of the Justice Department on Baker to be brought to the White House and kept there. The Kennedys let Johnson know that Baker was an enemy. Therefore, any story breaking that carried a link between Johnson and Baker would put him in a vise, with the Kennedys tightening the screws. He did not want the Kennedys to think he had been associating all this time with their enemy.

Also, Johnson knew enough about Baker's activities so that he did not wish to have his own close friendship aired at that time. That would be a grave danger to the future career of Johnson as vice-president and possibly someday again as a candidate for president. Johnson was now vice-president of the nation, not just the Senate leader, and he could not afford to be linked in any way with Baker's enterprises.

Although I had always believed that Johnson himself never had any idea how much Bobby was doing or what, the indications are now that Johnson knew plenty. Still, he put no curb on Baker, although Johnson was his boss in the Senate.

It was accurate, I felt, to describe Baker as "a Johnson protégé" because it was mostly Johnson who had put Bobby into the position of power and had taught him such political tricks as how to count heads in a Senate Democratic conference so as to keep a man like Senator Ralph Yarborough of Texas off the Senate Appropriations Committee just because Johnson had always considered him an opponent.

The message was clear. Johnson wanted my story stopped at all costs, and he did not want me to write any more stories linking him to Baker as his protégé.

At first, I was flabbergasted at the nerve of Johnson and Jenkins to try to put over such outright intimidation. Then I was amazed that they thought I would be so snowed by their power that I would retract the story. I was also amazed that they felt they could deny the close relationship which had always existed between Johnson and Baker since they met. Not only did Baker still call Johnson "leader" whenever speaking of him, but Johnson's wish was Baker's to perform. I was aghast at the stupidity and naiveté of this latest of public relations capers by Johnson— to try to bottle up the Baker story by laying a heavy hand on me. I believe Johnson thought he could stop nearly all of my outlets, and thus shut me up and keep the story from getting out.

The thought that even at that moment my syndicate outlet, North American Newspaper Alliance in New York, was going to press with my story on the Baker-Hill suit and Baker's financial empire delighted me.

Of course, I did not tell Jenkins this. I was thoroughly familiar with Johnson's tactics in stopping publication of any story sent out by the late columnist Drew Pearson that was critical of Johnson.

As I arose to leave Jenkins, I turned and said, "Walter, don't you think you can stop this story—it's bigger than you think. You will not be able to keep it bottled up. Furthermore, I presume that you and Lyndon do not know of some of the activities of Baker, or else you would not be trying to protect him. Do you know that there is an abortion racket organized and working behind the scenes in the Senate? Many of these cases were the result of partying in

Washington by big Democratic party fund contributors, who, when they developed problems later, were subject to hints that they ought to continue their gifts to the party."

I reminded him that this was no place for the vice-president or Walter to be involved. "You cannot stop this story from getting out—it is just too big," I said.

Outside, I immediately telephoned NANA in New York to warn them of Johnson's fury. I thought I should, in all justice to them. A night caretaker editor said the story was already on the wire.

I was pleased to find out the next day that the *Des Moines Register and Tribune* carried it on their front page, September 18, 1963. South Carolina papers carried it a few days later.

The Des Moines paper was one of those I had contacted on the weekend, trying to get a bigger outlet than my Southwest regional ones. The Des Moines syndicate editor had said at that time if it was such a "big story," that his Washington man, Clark Mollenhoff, "would have written it." I said I did not know why he had not done so, but I had the story and apparently Mollenhoff didn't. Later, I learned that Clark had said, "I would not touch it because it is dirty rotten apples and when you stir dirty rotten apples, you get dirtied."

Well, I guess Mollenhoff was surprised to read the story on the front page of his own paper the following Tuesday.

I knew the Waco and Austin papers, both supervised by Harry Provence, would not carry the story. The *San Antonio Light*, a Hearst newspaper, might have, but since I was a regional reporter, I steered away from the national scene with them. Still, I had a Texas angle here—Johnson.

Johnson had a very good friend from early congressional days in the Hearst higher echelon—Dick Berlin in New

York. Johnson often called him to ask favors. I did not wish to stir up action on that front.

The *El Paso Times*, which had a large circulation in New Mexico and some in Arizona as well as western Texas, had informed me that since this was a national story they wondered if they might be considered as acting with prejudice if they went out of their way to initiate a story so critical. They did not wish to seem outwardly abrasive to Johnson. El Paso is a long way from Washington, and the *Times* found it hard to believe that no other papers were interested in being first with this story.

I had an almost similar experience to the one I had in Des Moines when I contacted the *Chicago Tribune* service. They did not believe that there could be a big story here and that their own man at the Capitol, Willard Edwards, had not written it. They said they would wait for Willard's version. True, Willard was one of the most capable reporters at the Capitol, but he had not heard this story. One reason may have been that some of his longtime friends in the Senate—men like the late Senator Styles Bridges, Republican of New Hampshire, and the late Senator Everett Dirksen, Republican of Illinois—had been close friends and, at times, collaborators with Baker. No criticism of Edwards is intended here. It was just that his sources would not have "blown the whistle" on Baker.

Andy Glass, then covering the Senate for the *New York Herald Tribune*, said, "I am not writing about it and I certainly hope I will not have to cover the story. Bobby has given us many good leads on stories."

Baker had been particularly nice to the southern press, and was a great source of news to South Carolina, Tennessee, and Mississippi correspondents.

The Associated Press and the United Press were not

writing a thing about it. It was fully a month before they started covering it.

The *New York Times* waited almost six weeks before they began working on the story.

The *Washington Post* was desirous, I was told, of having someone else print the Baker story following up their brief first account of the suit filed by Hill against Baker. Why the editors desired this, I do not know, unless it was to take the heat off the paper, which daily had to deal with officials around the Senate, including Baker's office and his associates.

(The *Post* first carried the story on Hill's filing his lawsuit against Baker because it thought it was on the trail of a story that would hit at "Johnny Mack," Representative John McMillan, Democrat from South Carolina, who was chairman of the District of Columbia Committee and long the target of Washington blacks, press, and officials. He was often called "the mayor" of Washington. There had been previous stories of how Hill was working through his office in an attempt to get his vending machines into Washington offices.)

But the *Post* actually began to accumulate information for a big story. They sent their reporter Jack Landau to the Midwest to interview editors of the trade magazine in the vending machine field about Hill and Baker and the extensive racket of putting vending machines into defense plants as Baker was trying to do through forming of his Serv-U Corporation. The *Post*'s first investigative story on Baker came fourteen days after the first meager announcement of the Hill suit.

The other big Washington paper, the *Star*, began to follow the matter. But it was some time later that the two major Washington papers began to put teams of reporters on the story. Finally the *Star*'s crime expert, Miriam **Ot-tenberg**, was added to the Senate staff to work on this.

Laurence Stern of the *Post*, Paul Hope and John Barron of the *Star*, and Julian Morrison of the *Washington Daily News* were largely the ones who deserve the thanks of citizens for getting out to the nation as much of the story as the committee developed and they could dig up. Had the committee been able to open more doors to provide a record for quoting in the press, the people doubtless would know more today.

Reporters like Clark Mollenhoff were finally spending their full time covering the story. This was great because Clark in particular found some angles that others did not.

By this time, being a regional news reporter myself, I had to leave the story to cover more mundane news events for my regular newspapers. Nevertheless, with my background in the case I was able to get a few additional exclusives, which I sent to North American Newspaper Alliance. One of those was on the federal grand jury's investigation of the alleged abortion ring operating in and about the U.S. Capitol.

So diligent did the teams of local reporters become that the Raymond Clapper Award for outstanding reporting in the interests of crusading for the public interest was awarded to Stern and Barron that year.

One must also acknowledge the work of Jim McCartney of the *Chicago Daily News*, who wrote the story that Baker had said he held the votes of some ten senators in the palm of his hand.

But no one even then did anything about Baker. That was in April. Until September, he was left in his job with clout, influence, an office in the Capitol, and power to wield.

One of the most potentially damaging witnesses in the Baker investigation was Fred Black, the Washington lobbyist for the North American Aviation Corporation, one of the largest companies that did business with the government. North American Aviation had been awarded many aerospace and defense contracts, including the contract for the Apollo moon shot. It was alleged that Baker had offered to obtain lucrative contracts for Black's employer, North American, if Black, in turn, gave Baker's Serv-U Corporation the franchise to install its automatic vending machines in North American plants and in the plants of North American's subcontractors across the country.

In a separate government action, Black had been convicted of income tax evasion and sentenced to prison. But the case was appealed by him, finally reaching the Supreme Court. Later, after the Supreme Court found there was evidence gathered through electronic surveillance, the case was remanded by the Supreme Court to the lower court for retrial. The controversial evidence gained by wiretapping was ordered taken out. Then Black was found not guilty and was released, after five years of litigation. However, while the case was still on appeal, Black felt there was a possibility he might go to jail and he did not want to go alone. He made an appointment to tell everything he knew about Bobby Baker's activities to Senator Williams, the Delaware Republican who was investigating Baker and who had kept the investigation going in the Senate almost single-handedly. Black promised Williams he would name names. Since the name of Lyndon Johnson was sure to be among those mentioned, Black's announcement led to one of the busiest weekends Lyndon Johnson ever had.

Johnson had become president by the time Fred Black

threatened to embarrass and possibly to implicate him in
the growing Baker scandal, and he used all the power of
the White House to avoid getting involved. Soon after
Johnson became president, Bobby Kennedy was replaced
as attorney general by Nicholas Katzenbach, a Kennedy
holdover but a man with whom Johnson never felt at ease
during his years in the Justice Department. Johnson and
his closest adviser, Abe Fortas, both felt that the new attorney general, Katzenbach's replacement, should be a man
of unquestioned loyalty to Johnson. After all, there were
important matters to be dealt with in the Justice Department concerning the Bobby Baker case. Katzenbach chose
to take a demotion in the cabinet, down to under secretary
of state. I was immediately suspicious, and I'm afraid it
showed. The White House press staff sent me a set of pictures taken at that press conference, showing me with a
look of total amazement on my face. Marvin Watson, then
one of Johnson's White House aides, told me, "We figured
you knew something the others didn't." A set of these pictures is now in the Lyndon Johnson Library in Austin,
Texas.

Johnson decided he wanted Ramsey Clark to be his new
attorney general. Ramsey was the son of Johnson's longtime friends, former Attorney General and now Associate
Supreme Court Justice Tom Clark and his wife, Mary.
Johnson and Ramsey understood each other and seemed to
work well together. But, obviously, it would not do for an
attorney general who had supervision over so many cases
going on appeal to the Supreme Court to be taking these
matters before the court with the father of the attorney
general sitting on the bench. When this was broached to
the father, the elder Clark immediately offered to resign
from the highest court in the land, although holding that

position must have meant a great deal to him. Without hesitation or complaint, as Ramsey Clark told it in his eulogy of his father at memorial services in 1977, Tom Clark stepped down from the court to permit his son to become attorney general.

Now Johnson had a friend at the Justice Department. Many problems were shaping up in this period, one of the greatest being the demonstrations caused by the Vietnam War. Clark had to handle these delicately. The question of civil rights and private rights was gaining greater prominence in the courts, and certainly at the Justice Department.

During this period, Abe Fortas was perhaps the principal person on whom Johnson relied for advice. He knew the entire Bobby Baker story, as well as other incidents in Johnson's life. Johnson and Fortas were much worried when they were informed that Baker's associate, Fred Black, said he was going to see Senator John Williams of Delaware and tell all he knew.

Confidential files of the FBI on the Black case were examined, and they revealed that Black and his conversations with his attorney had been listened to by the FBI through bugging. That violated Black's civil rights. It was decided that it was only proper that the solicitor general of the Justice Department, then Thurgood Marshall, the outstanding black lawyer who had fought for civil rights in courts from Texas to Washington, should be the one to acknowledge this violation of civil rights by the government. For what was probably the first time in history, the American people saw a solicitor general "confess" in open court that the Justice Department had been guilty of illegal wiretapping while seeking to gather evidence against Black.

The effect—of throwing the Black case back to the lower courts—was immediate. That was the end of the Black case, and Black never kept his appointment with Senator Williams.

Eventually, Marshall was appointed by President Johnson to fill the vacancy on the Supreme Court.

Luckily for the American people, not all the evidence against Bobby Baker was kept secret, and he was forced to resign. He was indicted on an income tax charge, and was sent to jail after years of trials and appeals. Baker served a short sentence in Allenwood, which has been described as the country club of prisons. After he was released, Baker returned to Washington, where he reopened his office and renewed international and domestic business activities.

Before Baker went to jail, during his long legal battle, the White House continued to try to protect him and to cover up many questionable facets of his association with Johnson. A public relations campaign was launched to link Baker with Senator Kerr of Oklahoma to take some of the heat off Johnson by having someone else responsible for sponsoring Baker. Actually, it was Johnson who first brought Kerr and Baker together. Baker once tried to borrow money for one of his investments from LBJ. Johnson sent him to see Kerr, known to be a wealthy man. Kerr was a little surprised, as he thought of Baker as a canny vote counter on money issues, but, as any good banker would, he looked into Baker's proposal. Kerr must have decided Baker was a good risk, because Baker's name soon appeared on the list of stockholders of Kerr's bank in Oklahoma City.

But Kerr and Baker were never the close friends and business partners the White House tried to make them appear. Lyndon was using the press again: This time, through careful "leaks" to Drew Pearson, he exaggerated

Kerr and Baker's relationship to create some distance between himself and the former page. Later, Pearson was rewarded with many an exclusive story straight from the Oval Office. That was how Johnson worked.

Once Johnson became president, he stepped up his efforts to manage the press. Johnson often wrote Monday morning's newspaper headlines himself. How? His technique involved nothing more complicated than good timing. In Washington, few developments important enough to rate a front-page headline happen over the weekend (Nixon's "Saturday Night Massacre" was a major exception to this rule). Johnson, whose appetite for headlines was voracious, had his press secretary, George Reedy, during the Senate years, feed stories to copy-hungry reporters on Saturday, just after the Sunday morning news sections were well filled. Of course, the stories that resulted were always favorable to Johnson or critical of his enemies. In the White House, Johnson continued using his technique successfully.

Poor George Reedy! Working for Johnson was tough in any capacity, but it was impossible for this ethical press secretary to please both LBJ and the press. George was a nice person, and all he ever wanted to be was a good newspaperman. But because of Lyndon's desire for secrecy and his desire to control the press, LBJ made George's job so hard that he ended up hating it. He quit, but was persuaded to come back (no one ever got away from Johnson without a fight, and very few got away permanently at all). He soon wanted to leave again so badly that it was announced he needed foot surgery, and Johnson gave the job to George Christian, a newspaper and public relations man from Austin, Texas.

Bill Moyers, who had been a Peace Corps official, also

acted as Johnson's press secretary for a while, but he was not the ideal passer of information. He was always interpreting Lyndon, giving us his own opinion instead of that of his boss. We wanted to know what Johnson thought, not what Bill Moyers thought he thought.

Johnson should have been a reporter himself. He had a remarkable memory and a great sense of what was news. He always tried to write the lead paragraph for reporters when he gave us a story, and some reporters fell for this maneuver and used his leads. Johnson was his own best press secretary.

When it came to news reporters (or staff, or even friends), Johnson had his momentary pets and, like the crowned heads of France, saved his attention, secrets, and favors for these special friends.

One of Johnson's great favorites was William S. White, a newspaperman from De Leon, Texas. They met in Washington at the beginning of Johnson's career when Lyndon was a clerk to a Texas congressman. White was working for the Associated Press at the time, and came by the Congressman's office every day, trying to get a story. Johnson later used his influence to help White become a syndicated columnist, every newsman's dream assignment. When Johnson was president, White, who wrote for United Features syndicate, came by the White House every day to get material for his column. He became known as the "Johnson voice." In a similar way, Johnson helped Marianne Means of the Hearst newspapers to turn out many an analytical column.

Johnson was not as free with stories to less favored reporters. I remember being part of a group of newspaper and broadcast reporters waiting outside Lyndon's hotel room at a Democratic national convention in Chicago while inside, behind a closed door, LBJ was giving an exclusive interview to Scotty Reston of the *New York Times*. Talk about professional jealousy! The interview went on and on; the door stayed closed. Mary McGrory of the *Washington Evening Star* got so tired of waiting that she went out to sit on the fire escape high above the city. But I got angry. In fact, I was so mad that I went to the front door and kicked it as hard as I could. Then I ran back and hid behind Peter Kumpa of the *Baltimore Sun*, the tallest reporter present. Lyndon opened the door, saw Peter standing there first in line, scowled at us, closed the door again, and continued talking to Reston. But our maneuver worked. A minute later, Reston came out. He was scowling, too.

Although Lyndon and I went back a long way together, we seldom had a chance to talk after he became president. When Johnson was in the Senate, he wanted me around "to give me good coverage," he said, or at least to write about him back in Texas. I covered him regularly when he was in the House and Senate, and accompanied him on many trips. But when Johnson moved to the White House, his activities were covered in detail by the wire services, and everyone read about him everywhere. Johnson no longer needed my stories, and after the Bobby Baker story, he was furious with me.

Just the same, I felt no antagonism toward him. And when I wanted to tell him something, I still would do so by memorandum, which I placed with someone to get it to him by hand. Once I wrote him about how dirty and hot were the slums where black people lived around 6th and R streets and elsewhere in Northwest Washington. I asked him to go look and then do something about it. The next day I ran into him coming out of a Texas delegation luncheon at the Capitol. He stopped to talk and said, "Your memo was on my night reading stand last night." I was gratified.

Our relationship, which had many emotional ups and downs in the past, fell apart when I said in print that Bobby Baker was Johnson's protégé. After I broke the Baker story (Johnson was still vice-president), he turned down my requests for interviews again and again. He finally agreed to see me for a few minutes once, but when I got to his office and started asking questions, he sat at his desk signing letters and never once looked up. His only answers were "yes" and "no," which are almost worthless to a reporter trying to get a story. I was so hurt, so stymied by his attitude, that tears came to my eyes, and my voice broke. "If that's the way you treat old friends . . . ," I said as I walked out of the room. It was one of the few times in my life when I cried on the job. That was in October, 1963. By November, Johnson was in the White House.

Three days after Johnson became president, I received a call from Harry Provence. Provence said that I had lost my Austin and Waco accounts—the two biggest papers in central Texas—to Les Carpenter, another Texas correspondent. LBJ "didn't want to worry about critical stories coming from you," Provence told me. I could keep my smaller accounts—I had another paper in Lufkin, in the piney woods, and one on the Gulf Coast, at Port Arthur— and I could still earn the same amount of money I earned when I wrote for all four papers. Les Carpenter had insisted on that, Provence told me.

The Carpenters got involved with Johnson when they first arrived in Washington from Texas. LBJ was their congressman, and Les and his wife, Liz, went to Johnson to ask his help in getting established, obtaining stories, and making contacts. It was just the sort of assignment Johnson relished. The three of them understood each other and got along very well. As it turned out, I was the one who got Les Carpenter his first job in Washington. I tipped him off about an upcoming vacancy in Bascom Timmons's office, where I was working at the time, when Les just arrived in Washington, complaining about a back injury and carrying a fresh navy discharge. But that did not make Les feel grateful toward me. By the time Johnson was president, Liz was Lady Bird's press secretary. When Les took over my accounts, he didn't even have to bother going to the White House to get a story.

I had known the Carpenters for years, and this was not the first time one or both of them collided with me. Soon after Liz and Les arrived in Washington, she called to ask if they could be invited to a reception I was holding for some Texas congressmen. It was a very small party in a small house. My entertainment budget was so tight that I just couldn't invite them. From then on, the Carpenters thought of me as an enemy. They told Drew Pearson that I was a hard-line conservative, which wasn't true, but, thanks to them, I was labeled a conservative for years, which hurt me and limited my effectiveness as a newspaper reporter. When people ask me if I'm a liberal or a conservative, a Republican or a Democrat, I always say I'm a newspaper reporter. But if I have to have a label, call me a populist. I'm more interested in people's individual rights than in what party they belong to or which political philosophy they subscribe to.

The Carpenters apparently thought that LBJ didn't like me (not always true) but liked them better. We were different. They said he didn't want me around, and especially didn't want me to attend any social functions that involved him. That was totally not true. I know for a fact he was fond of me. I thought I lost a lot of stories because of this myth.

I also lost an account to Les when three executives from my Beaumont paper came to see me in "my" office at the National Press Building. Since I was a woman and therefore at the time not a member of the National Press Club (the first women were admitted in 1971; I worked twenty-seven years to become a member), I was forced to share an office with two or three male reporters. On the day the publisher and two editors from Beaumont came to see me, Sally was visiting. It was the day of the pre-Christmas Santa Claus Parade downtown. When they walked into the crowded room, she was sitting on my lap, the only place to sit in the room. There wasn't even enough room for them to stand. Then they noticed a big, freshly painted office with only one tenant down the hall. It was Les Carpenter's new office, and they took the Beaumont account away from me and gave it to him.

After Les died in 1974, Liz finally went back to Austin. She arranged a very fancy farewell party for herself before she left Washington. Everybody in town was invited— except, of course, me. Right to the very end, Liz *never* forgave me for saying no to her.

I was not the only newspaper reporter to find out that Johnson could love you one day and hate you the next. I even saw Lyndon Johnson get angry at Tex Easley, the original mild-mannered reporter, who covered Washington for eighty-five Texas newspapers—a man who went out of his way not to print anything derogatory about anyone. In contrast, I felt it was my patriotic duty to expose everything I saw and heard.

For some reason, even the relationship between Johnson and Harry Provence seemed to cool during Johnson's White House years. Provence, who had been a frequent caller, was around the White House less and less. Provence denies that anything happened, but I found him seated in a corner of the gallery with other reporters at Johnson's funeral, while close friends sat with the family, by invitation.

Johnson's attempts to manipulate the media did not stop with newspapers. His power over the television and radio stations in Texas was absolute. His influence with the national networks was formidable. Although Johnson's station in Austin was a CBS affiliate, all three networks did many favors for Johnson and gave him plenty of coverage. They also sought out his advice when they created new network affiliates in his home state. I remember one Texas station owner, a boss of mine, who believed that Johnson stood between him and network approval. He had been on the phone with Walter Jenkins for weeks trying to get an appointment to see LBJ. When he finally flew to Washington, the station owner found that LBJ was at the Mayo Clinic in Minnesota, where he was scheduled for surgery.

My boss did another thing to offset Johnson's tight control over who would get an extension of a network affiliation in Texas. He went to see Speaker Sam Rayburn about it. He told Mr. Sam what Lyndon was doing. Mr. Sam was shocked and said Lyndon had no right to be doing anything like that and he would speak to Lyndon. Apparently he did.

I was having lunch with my former boss at the rooftop restaurant of the Washington Hotel when a call came through from Lady Bird, who was at her husband's bedside. She told him Lyndon had agreed and that he would get his network affiliation approved. There would be no further interference. No more interference—the station owner gave a huge sigh of relief.

Johnson created and preserved a television monopoly at

KTBC in Austin for years by keeping competitive television stations out of the market. Finally, some city fathers decided Austin needed more than one network station. Richard Brown, a nephew of the Fentress family and the head of its Austin newspaper, was tired of Johnson's heavyhanded control, tired of hearing people say that Johnson called the shots on the *Austin American-Statesman*. Brown was a strong, independent man, the heir to vast newspaper interests, who, unlike Provence, was not willing to accept the same policy of surrender to Johnson as his uncle, Harlon Fentress. Furthermore, Brown was tired of being the butt of jokes. People in Austin said if Johnson coughed, the Fentress papers in Austin, Waco, Port Arthur, and Lufkin would come running with a bottle of medicine.

Brown came to Washington, determined to break LBJ's stranglehold on Austin television. But when Brown, Harry Provence, and I finally met with Johnson, LBJ did all the talking, as always, and Brown never got in a word. One of the things that Johnson told us at that meeting was that Ralph Yarborough, the Democratic senator from Texas, had received a $200,000 campaign contribution from Billie Sol Estes. After consulting with my editor in Texas, we ran this story, which brought instant denials from the hopelessly frustrated Yarborough, who claims to be innocent to this day. (No matter: He lost the election.) Johnson told us not to reveal that he was the source of the story, but I am sure Yarborough knew all along that he had been done in by his old political enemy.

Looking back, I am beginning to believe Yarborough when he says that this story was but another of the many dirty tricks Johnson played on him. Texas politics can be quite complicated.

When Johnson became president and needed solid support, he appealed to Yarborough's sense of cooperation and got it. But when Johnson had been majority leader, I watched LBJ and Bobby Baker personally steer a place on the important Senate Appropriations Committee from Ralph Yarborough to William Proxmire, a Democrat from Wisconsin. Some of Johnson's Senate colleagues would have disowned him if they had known this; they disliked Proxmire, a maverick newcomer who dared to criticize some of the established go-alongs on the committee. Anyone looked better to Johnson than Yarborough, though.

Although Yarborough and Johnson were both Democrats from Texas, they were real opposites when it came to personality and philosophy. Yarborough, the liberal, was a visionary with a true love for and desire to serve ordinary people. Yarborough came from a town fifteen miles out of Tyler. He was a poor boy, and I remember seeing him bring his lunch to high school in Tyler in a tin pail. The McClendons, who considered themselves the town aristocrats, really looked down their noses at that. Johnson, more conservative than Yarborough, tried to be a good friend to rich, powerful, and influential businessmen. Lyndon found every way in the world to play dirty tricks on Yarborough. I was in Johnson's office when Yarborough, newly arrived in Washington, came by to pledge his cooperation. Lyndon acted friendly, but later he never missed a chance to stab Yarborough in the back.

Billie Sol Estes, the man Johnson said gave Yarborough $200,000, was one of the strangest characters ever to appear on the American scene. Marge Carpenter (no relation to Les and Liz), a Pecos, Texas, newswoman, was sent by her editor to count the fertilizer tanks that had been the basis of Estes's business empire. Marge found that these tanks existed only in Estes's imagination and credit applications. When Marge interviewed Estes, he told her that his ambition was to get a corner on the world grain market. Once he controlled the world's supply of grain, Estes alone would decide which starving people he would sell to. The future of the world would be in Billie Sol's hands. Marge said Estes's favorite photograph showed him pointing to a globe. He was proud of his middle name, Sol, the Spanish word for sun. She found his remarks shocking, even frightening. To Marge, Estes was a paranoid little man whose voice became high and shrill when he described his vision of power. When she returned to her newspaper after the interview, she actually threw up.

When Estes was running for election to the local school board, Marge's paper, the *Pecos Independent*, endorsed his opponent. After he lost the election, Estes took revenge on the *Independent* by starting his own paper, the *Daily News*. He planned to run the older paper out of town. This effort was the beginning of the end for Estes. The *Independent* started a low-key campaign against him. First, they published a series of four front-page articles on his business activities. Although Estes was never mentioned by name in these articles, there was little doubt about who was involved. His name was not mentioned because Estes was so popular among townspeople and pressures in his favor were high. Copies of these articles were sent to the finance companies that did business with Billie Sol, and they sent their representatives to Pecos to investigate. When they got to town, they found that the fertilizer tanks, which had been the sole basis of Estes's collateral for millions of dollars of credit, were nonexistent.

Eventually, charges were filed aganst Estes. He was arrested, and after he was out of business, the town of Pecos began to realize that Estes had been their main industry. Suddenly, Pecos was an angry town. Townspeople began to blame the newspaper for breaking the story in the first place. They blamed Marge for exposing the fact that the tanks didn't exist. Before the newspaper articles were published, the fact that the tanks did not exist had hardly been a secret in Pecos. When Marge Carpenter told her husband, a banker, that there were no tanks, he laughed at her and told her that the bankers in town knew that. It was the newspaper stories that blew the lid off Estes's wheeling and dealing.

Marge was practically run out of town. Her husband started drinking, lost his job, and committed suicide. Her father came for the funeral and had a stroke. Estes's newspaper merged with the *Independent* and Marge lost her job. All this happened in a matter of weeks since her interview with Billie Sol. With three children to support, Marge moved to another town. She lived in a trailer, accepted whatever small reporting jobs she could find, and saw her children on weekends. Although the Estes story was a personal disaster for Marge, professionally she was never sorry for one minute that she helped expose Billie Sol Estes.

The secretary of agriculture did not share Marge's attitude, however. Nor did any of his top bureaucrats, who had hobnobbed with Estes for years, as had staff members of the Democratic National Committee. Now they collaborated to cover up as much of the mess in the Department of Agriculture as possible.

Some highly conservative Democrats in Congress did little to expose these manipulations. Representative L. H. Fountain of North Carolina, chairman of a House Government Operations subcommittee, fired a committee lawyer, Robert Manuel, for "leaking" a report to the *New York Herald Tribune* that the Department of Agriculture had been trying to keep from a Texas grand jury. The committee seemed more interested in finding out how the news about Estes's manipulations of cotton allotments and about his influence in the department was leaked to the press than they were in uncovering the rest of the mess. I called the committee myself to ask why certain big East Coast papers had the leaked report when I, a Texas reporter, did not. This amazed Robert Manuel, who said in the printed committee hearing report: "Sarah McClendon's resentment was not because I had leaked the report, but because I had not leaked it to her." Quite true. "She covered the farmers," Manuel continued, "and she had not had her share of the goodies." Absolutely.

The investigators found that Billie Sol's main business had been selling other people's credit, sometimes without their knowledge. Billie Sol paid rent on the tanks to these farmers just as if the tanks really existed. Estes was a generous man. Besides paying "rent" to cooperative farmers, it was proved that Billie Sol treated certain members of the Department of Agriculture to new wardrobes from Neiman-Marcus. One of these well-dressed bureaucrats, William E. Morris, was fired outright by Agriculture Secretary Orville Freeman. Luckily, his wife had a job. She was the Washington correspondent for Estes's newspaper, the *Pecos Daily News*.

Estes's generosity did not stop with giving gifts to the staff of the Department of Agriculture. Jerry Holleman, assistant secretary of labor, was criticized for accepting Estes's contribution of $1,000 for a dinner that Labor Secretary Arthur Goldberg was giving for Lyndon Johnson. It was no wonder that Ralph Yarborough was upset and angry when he was accused of accepting a contribution from Estes. Representative H. Karl Anderson, a Minnesota Republican, had been considered an ethical man, but when it was revealed that Anderson had accepted Estes's money, he was a political goner.

Although he seemed to know everyone in Texas and Washington, somehow or other, Billie Sol had stayed far away from me. I heard of him for the first time when Marge's story broke. (Unfortunately, it was not Marge who got to write the crowning story. After discovering the missing tanks, she had turned over all her facts to her editors. They decided to hold off for a time. Then the story was assigned to Oscar Griffin to develop. He won the Pulitzer Prize. He did offer to share it with Marge, but she declined to take any of the money.) Then I discovered that Estes had been purposely avoiding my path. He once "confided" to his forty or fifty dinner guests from the Department of Agriculture (Billie Sol liked large and frequent parties) that he didn't want to come anywhere near me. I guess he had too much to hide to face my questions. My daughter, Sally, was once invited to accompany one of Estes's guests to a $100-a-plate fund raiser. When Sally found out that Estes had paid for every seat at the table, she returned home and said, "Mother, I think you better watch that man."

Another Texan in Washington said he had never heard of Estes until his name became national news. That was Vice-President Lyndon Johnson. A week or two after Sally's hundred-dollar dinner, LBJ decided to hold a big reception at his home, the Elms, which he had bought from Perle Mesta. Charles Boatner of Fort Worth, Johnson's press aide at the time, said that Johnson was first introduced to Estes at that reception. Johnson didn't quite get Estes's name when they were introduced, and he called him Willie Joe all afternoon. Boatner told that story with a straight face, but I didn't believe a word of it.

Of course, those autographed pictures that Estes had up on his wall from President Kennedy, Vice-President Johnson, and others could have been arranged without the knowledge of the people who were pictured. After all, Estes was a heavy contributor to the Democratic party. He certainly tried to give the impression that he knew many powerful people in Washington. He had shown Marge Carpenter snapshots of himself and his wife, Patsy, at a table at President John F. Kennedy's Inaugural Ball. Seated with the couple were Vice-President and Mrs. Lyndon Johnson and House Speaker John W. McCormack of Massachusetts. Marge said that Estes wanted to be Kennedy's secretary of agriculture. Instead, with Ralph Yarborough's help, he was offered membership on the Cotton Advisory Committee of that department.

I attended some sessions of the Estes hearing in Washington, and I was shocked to hear officials who had once cooperated with Estes try to block the investigation. But one thing really convinced me that a cover-up was going on at the Department of Agriculture. Certain staff employees tried to have an employee named Mary Jones committed to a mental institution, and might have succeeded, had it not been for two friends of mine, Grace Johnson and Jane Rollins, who persuaded me to act on my own to help her.

Mary Jones worked as an assistant to N. Battle Hales, a staff member of the department. In the normal course of their duties, the two of them happened to be in possession of the Estes file on his manipulation of cotton allotments, fertilizer tanks, and cotton advisory activities. This file included all the facts on illegal cotton allotments and on nonexistent fertilizer tanks. It also contained letters that could prove embarrassing to many people around the department. Both Mary and her boss were sure that certain officials would try to "borrow" the file. They feared that changes or deletions might be made in it. Perhaps a letter or two would get "lost." Mary Jones and her boss refused to let the file leave their office.

But when Mary came to work one morning, she found her boss had been transferred. Hales was feeling the brunt of adverse personnel action. A staff man was in the process of removing Estes's file. Mary Jones stood in front of the door and announced that she would not move. If Mary had anything to say about it, that file would not leave her office. But she was literally dragged, kicking and screaming, down the hall. En route, she lost a shoe. She was taken to the office of the department's doctor, who called the Washington, D.C., Police Department to come get her and take her to the mental ward of D.C. General Hospital.

The police didn't question the doctor's authority, put Mary into a straitjacket, and took her to the hospital, where she was forcibly detained for observation in the psychiatric ward. She was kept there for weeks, this small woman who merely wanted to do her job. It was the Department of Agriculture that was crazy.

When friends told me what had happened to this poor woman, I tried to see the doctor who sent her to the hospital. The Department of Agriculture would not let me near him. I asked several times about Mary's case, but was given the impression that she was a distraught woman who was mentally ill. I learned that there was going to be a sanity hearing for Mary Jones, but that no witnesses were scheduled to testify for Mary. My two friends pleaded with me to do something to free her. They were afraid that she would be confined there for the rest of her life.

They suggested that I contact Frederick Heath, then a deputy director of public health in Washington who often acted as chief of the District of Columbia Health Department on weekends. He was a quiet, sensitive person who took his weekend appointment seriously and used his authority well. He was highly sensitive to public opinion, and Mary's friends believed he would be responsive to pressure from the press. I didn't know Mr. Heath, but I called him at his home one Saturday night to say that other newspaper reporters and I were watching the case, and that we intended to report whether or not Mary Jones would be represented by counsel and have defense witnesses during her hearing that next Monday. I did know that other reporters were interested. Heath had never heard of Mary, but he said he would look into the matter and take care of it. He did. At the hearing, Mary had a lawyer and her former boss was there to speak up for her. Instead of being routinely sent off to a hospital as Agriculture Department officials thought she would be, Mary was paroled to the custody of her family in Arlington, Virginia, and was later given her freedom.

Agriculture Secretary Orville Freeman had scheduled a press conference to take place shortly after Mary's hearing was due to end. But suddenly the press conference was delayed for an hour. When it finally did take place, Freeman had nothing to say about Mary Jones or the file she tried to protect. I never did find out exactly what information was hidden in that file. But enough evidence existed outside the secret files of the Department of Agriculture to send Estes to prison for years. The whole experience made me wonder how many other government employees might have had a similar experience. Perhaps not all of them were lucky enough to escape.

I was later told that there have been numerous cases in government bureaucracy of women with idiosyncrasies (or perhaps just an untidy personal appearance) who have been nudged out of jobs into hospitals or early retirement to suit the wishes of superiors.

# 8

## *LBJ Manages People*

Johnson was as addicted to fads and impulses in his relations with his staff as he was to picking temporary favorites in the news field. At times, he would sour on some staff
member and banish him or her from his presence to a back-
room operation, where that staffer was expected to remain
loyal and wait patiently for another day. It often dawned.
After years, Juanita Roberts became a top secretary at the
White House and helped found the Johnson Library at
Austin.

But whether a staff member was in favor or disfavor,
once a Johnson employee, always a Johnson employee. If
former employees didn't volunteer to return in times of
crisis, such as when President Kennedy was killed, they
were called back. Bill Moyers, who first worked as Johnson's traveling secretary-valet, didn't like his job. He finally
convinced Johnson to let him join the Peace Corps, where
he felt he would be happier and more effective. But when
Johnson became president, Moyers was back on staff, acting
as LBJ's appointments secretary and later as press secretary
to the new president.

Even Walter Jenkins, LBJ's closest aide since Senate
days, tried to leave Johnson once. Marjorie Jenkins, Walter's

wife, was tired of Walter's long hours, tired of raising five children in a small house. She convinced Walter to take the family home to Texas. But after a few months, Lyndon called Walter to say that he had found them a new, larger house. Coincidentally, the house was in Lyndon's own neighborhood, which tied Walter to him more closely than ever.

Walter was one of the most efficient men I have ever come across in government. He was also one of the kindest, most considerate, and most cooperative. He was a man of considerable power, but he never used this power to his own personal advantage. He worked his staff as hard as LBJ worked him, but he also planned picnics, baseball games, and poker sessions for them. If someone needed help or a job recommendation, Walter was the man to see. When the need arose, he even acted as a marriage counselor. He was also a devoted husband, father, and a good friend. Whenever my daughter, Sally, spent the night with Lynda Byrd at the Johnsons' home, it was always Walter whom Johnson summoned to pick up Sally on Sunday morning to take her to church with his family. (He converted to Catholicism, a happy surprise for his wife, Marjorie.)

Jenkins had an encyclopedic mind, especially when it came to people. He expedited solutions to literally thousands of problems during his twenty-five-year tenure as Johnson's chief aide. I've heard it said that Jenkins knew everyone on Capitol Hill, and it may very well have been true. He knew more people than anyone else in Washington, and he always knew whom to ask for help. Jenkins could solve most problems with one or two phone calls.

He was the only person in the White House who could actually speak for the president. And he always knew where he could reach the boss.

The Walter Jenkins scandal was one of the saddest chapters in Washington history. What made Jenkins's case particularly newsworthy (and tragic) was its timing. At the time the scandal hit the headlines, Jenkins was number two man in the White House, just as Sherman Adams had been in Eisenhower's time. Walter was unquestionably Lyndon's strong right arm, officially and personally. He was the president's link to White House personnel, the civil service, the family business (Jenkins did Johnson's taxes), and the press.

I knew both Walter and Marjorie Jenkins quite well and spotted them at a late Sunday afternoon Mass to which many Washington officials came at the Immaculate Conception Church at 8th and N streets, NW. It was the Sunday before tragedy struck this family.

During the service, the priest kept asking for more money and passing the plate. I kept contributing. Then I discovered I did not have carfare home. I asked Walter and Marjorie for a ride. They agreed to drive me home if I wasn't in a hurry. I wasn't. They had to drive to the White House first to check Walter's messages. When we got there, the list of people who had called in the hour or two since Walter last checked read like *Who's Who*. There had been calls from Secretary of Commerce Luther Hodges, from James Farley in New York (FDR's political adviser and postmaster general), from Henry Ford, and from the head of a large newspaper chain. They all knew that if they couldn't get Lyndon Johnson on the phone, the man to talk to was Walter Jenkins, who could give a straight answer. They knew that whatever Walter told them was truthful and accurate. People could depend on him. Johnson did.

I talked to Marjorie that afternoon in the White House about her husband's important role in running the country.

She looked at me and said, "Life is moving so fast for us."

The next day, a friend called to try to tell me that Walter had been arrested several days before for allegedly indecent homosexual behavior in the YMCA men's room. The story had just broken. But I interrupted my friend before he could tell me the story. I told him instead about my exciting afternoon at the White House with the powerful and successful Walter Jenkins. My friend, distraught over my enthusiasm, quickly got off the phone without telling me the news. I flew to Fort Worth that afternoon to cover an airplane story, and it wasn't until after I arrived that I heard Walter was in the hospital. I couldn't imagine what was wrong, so I called the White House, where a secretary covered for Walter and gave me no idea of the seriousness of the situation. Later that night, I called Sally, who was home in Washington. She was crying as if her heart would break. "Mother," she said, "they're saying the worst things about Mr. Jenkins on the radio. He's the man who used to drive me to church!"

As soon as I heard the whole story, I was no longer interested in General Dynamics airplanes. I needed to get back to Washington. On the flight back, I kept shaking my head in disbelief. I felt sick. Back home I found Walter in the hospital, not seeing visitors. Later, I was the first reporter allowed in his room. We were both calm and quiet during my visit, but we both knew there were terrible days ahead.

Hundreds of prominent people sent sympathetic messages to Jenkins. J. Edgar Hoover, a former neighbor, was one of the first to send flowers. Lady Bird loyally came forward to express to the nation her confidence and sympathy. Johnson ordered the FBI to investigate. But the public never found out what was in their report or why and how the incident occurred, and the Jenkins case has remained a great psychiatric and political mystery. It is still today the subject of speculation. Was it a politically motivated plot? Walter had been ill, was exhausted from overwork, and had been imbibing at a news media party. Recently I was reminded by his secretary, Dorothy Nichols: "That man was just too overworked—he worked so hard he had no time for off-duty pursuits."

The Jenkins family moved back to Austin, but Walter and Marjorie were still tied to the Johnsons. LBJ had paid all of Walter's hospital bills, and he and Lady Bird gave the family a beautiful lakeside lot they had been saving for their own retirement home. With Johnson's help, Jenkins went into public relations. His talent and efficient know-how were sorely missed at the White House.

Lady Bird knew her husband's passion for efficiency, and saw to it that his private life ran smoothly. She was one of the best housekeepers I ever saw. Her linen closet was like something out of a magazine, with each stack labeled and piled neatly. Her staff of maids and cooks were perfectly trained—nothing else would please Lyndon. Mrs. Johnson ought to be given much of the credit for her husband's successful career. She truly shared in his joys, sorrows, and accomplishments. My daughter, Sally, and I used to say, "Lady Bird is a saint—she would have to be to put up with Lyndon's temperament." He was lucky to have her.

It was Lady Bird, along with Zephyr Wright, the longtime faithful Johnson cook, who kept Lyndon alive after his first heart attack. Because of the attention these two women paid to LBJ's weight and diet, Johnson was able to survive his heart attack and handle the burdens of the Kennedy assassination, the presidency, his own campaign, and the Vietnam War. I remember seeing Lady Bird at the hospital feeding her husband cantaloupes, which were said to be high in bulk, low in calories, and good for LBJ at that time. Pecos County, Texas, was famous for its cantaloupes, and farmers there sent him bushels of them.

One day, when Johnson was a junior in the Senate, I was sitting in his office, trying to get a story. Lady Bird, home in Texas, had just lost a baby and was feeling quite depressed. There had been some question as to whether she would continue to live a political life with all its family upsets. I knew Lyndon was worried. As he and I talked about some government matter, he received a telegram, which he immediately read and passed over to me so that I could see it, too. The telegram was from Lady Bird and it said that she loved him dearly and would always be by his side. Lyndon was thrilled. I'm sure Lady Bird never dreamed that anyone but Lyndon would read that telegram, and I'm sure that Lyndon never told her that he'd shown it to me.

Johnson's office staff was expected to be not only highly efficient but always available for work. Johnson's secretaries were expected to stay on the job each day as long as LBJ needed their services, which was, more often than not, late into the night. It was very difficult for these women to have a home life or a social life. They had to break dates again and again. Time after time, Johnson demanded that his secretaries, even the women with small children, board an airplane and go on a trip with him on an hour's notice. Geraldine Williams, a former Johnson secretary and now the wife of newspaper columnist Bob Novak, could type faultlessly on an airplane and was the quickest clothes packer on the staff.

"Home" at the White House, Johnson's secretaries spent most of their time with the files or on the telephone. Johnson's files were all-encompassing, and were filled with the phone numbers of everyone Johnson needed to call, from heads of state to precinct leaders in Texas. He had a large corps of volunteer informers to help him keep the files current, especially in Texas. Old friends and allies would call Johnson or write to him to report any local Democrat who was seen sneaking off the reservation.

Johnson had a large, strong network. His telephone lists must have been volumes long. His secretaries were required to know how to reach LBJ's key people instantly and anyone else in a few minutes. Johnson might ask to speak to the governor of Utah or to a camel driver in Pakistan, and any secretary who could not produce was sure to be chewed out by her boss.

Johnson was never far from his private telephone list, even when he slept. When the press was invited to tour the president's own rooms in the White House, I looked until I spotted the telephone list. The black book was on a table beside the bed in Lady Bird's room. The president and his wife still slept together.

Johnson was as possessive and manipulative about the lives of his secretaries as he was about the lives of his aides. Mary Margaret Wylie, one of Johnson's favorite secretaries, had practically no life of her own when she worked for him. She worked day and night in his office when he was in Washington, and was expected to accompany him when he traveled. After Mary Margaret's marriage to Jack Valenti of Houston, whom she met through Johnson, the boss built a house for her on his lakeshore property. He called it Mary Margaret's house when he showed it to me and other reporters. But the Valentis stayed home in Houston. Mary Margaret said it was too far from Houston to Lake LBJ.

After the assassination of President Kennedy, Valenti,

who was an efficient public relations person and had been doing advance work for the Kennedy-Johnson ticket in Texas, came back to Washington with Johnson and went to work for him at the White House.

Valenti moved his family to Washington, and he, Mary Margaret, and their small daughter, Courtenay, who loved to call LBJ "prez," were frequently in attendance at the White House for social functions and private visits to the Oval Office.

Once Johnson picked up the daughter and perched her on his shoulder while going through the crowd of guests at a reception for top veterans affairs officials in the State Dining Room. When he came alongside me, he pointed to the child's curly head and said, "Sarah, see how much she looks like Jack!"

Mary Margaret had been part of the Johnson inner circle. Lyndon and Lady Bird literally shared the wealth with a faithful few when they created a profit-sharing plan. The money came from profits of the family broadcasting business in Austin. Along with Mary Margaret, I know the Walter Jenkinses were part of this profit-sharing group.

Johnson was a very generous man, and he loved giving presents to the people around him. He was very high on self-improvement, and for years he sent his wife and the wives of his close friends and staff members to New York so they could attend makeup and hairstyling courses to become more glamorous. He once said he'd sponsor a trip for me, but he never got around to it. Back in those days, I probably would have turned my nose up at such a project, but I've finally learned, thanks to my television and lecture appearances, that clothes and makeup can *help*.

Johnson once had every member of his extended "family"

who wore glasses fitted for contact lenses. When he noticed that my daughter, Sally (who was friendly with his daughter Lynda), had to wear her thick glasses constantly, he offered to have his own eye doctor fit her with contact lenses, too. At that time, I couldn't possibly afford to repay him. Johnson knew that and told me I could pay him back "when things get easier." Johnson deplored the sight of a pretty young girl wearing glasses.

LBJ once sent for me to ask why I had *not* come to him with an outright request for help in my search for a summer job for my nephew. Coming from a family with proud notions—remember, we thought of ourselves as too independent to ask a favor—had kept me from asking anyone's help. I knew that Johnson got requests every day for jobs and favors, and I didn't want to add to his burden. But Johnson told me he was shocked that I hadn't asked. "We all have our problems," he said. "I have a big family, and my folks are always needing something. I'll give your nephew a job. Tell him to see Walter." And soon my nephew was working long hours at the Capitol and on weekends playing baseball on the Jenkins team.

I was particularly touched by Lyndon's kindness when he took the time to speak to me after he heard I'd been in court following an automobile accident. "You have so much to do," he said sympathetically, "I don't know how in the world you do it all." That busy man actually took the time to acknowledge that I was working and raising and supporting a child alone. Of course, all this happened before I wrote the story about Bobby Baker.

The same taste for momentary favorites that Johnson displayed in his relationship with the press and with his staff seemed to guide him when it came to making staff appointments also. After Kennedy died, Johnson tried to keep on as many of the old Kennedy appointees as possible for the sake of appearance and of unity. Some of the men who stayed were types far removed from Johnson's usual colleagues, such as Richard Goodwin, Carl Rowan, and Walt Rostow. Johnson went out of his way to court the intellectual university types who had seemed so at ease with his predecessor. But many of these men brought him grief when they left him for greener pastures, making it clear that they considered the new president less than their equal. This was the same prejudice I encountered in Washington: How could someone from west of the Mississippi be as smart as someone from Boston? Boston is the most parochial city I know—no city in the South comes close. But people in Washington played down Lyndon Johnson's abilities and achievements. After all, Johnson was not a Kennedy person.

Some Kennedy men did stay around to become permanently identified with Johnson, such as Walt Rostow. When Rostow found he could not return to his previous job as an Ivy League professor because of his support for the war in Vietnam, LBJ, always loyal to those who stood by him, found him a job on the faculty of the University of Texas.

Of all the men and women Lyndon Johnson knew and worked with over the years in Washington, probably the most influential was Sam Rayburn. From Bonham, Texas, Rayburn was Speaker of the House of Representatives longer than anyone else and left Congress a legacy of rules and traditions that live today. He was a man who put his country first at all times. Nothing hurt him more than for someone to imply that he put the interests of the Democratic party before those of the United States. Rayburn frequently put partisan politics aside to help smooth relations between Congress and the White House. This man, who made and touched so much history from the day he came to Congress at age thirty-one in 1913 until his death on November 18, 1961, was a completely selfless patriot. And after the United States of America and the Democratic party, Rayburn loved the House of Representatives.

He really cared about people. Rayburn could remember only too well how it was back on the farm in the country, the only light coming from kerosene lamps. That is why he was such a champion of the Rural Electrification Act, which brought electricity to remote parts of our country.

I can think of two occasions when I believe that Rayburn single-handedly saved America. The first was the crucial vote on the military draft, which came up months before Pearl Harbor. There was a lot of opposition to the draft in the House. Military leaders said it was needed urgently. When the vote was taken, the measure passed by one vote. A re-vote was suggested, but Rayburn said it wouldn't be necessary; he had paid close attention and had an accurate vote count. If the draft had been voted down, our army would have been too small and too inexperienced to be effective after Pearl Harbor was attacked.

Later in the war, General George C. Marshall, chief of staff of the army and later secretary of defense, asked to meet with Speaker Rayburn on a matter of the utmost importance. Rayburn asked House Majority Leader John W. McCormack of Boston to meet with them. Secretary Henry Stimson also came along. Marshall requested that Congress give the Department of the Army (at that time there was no Defense Department) $2 billion without asking any questions about how the money was to be used.

Of course, in seeking funds from Congress, one had to go the usual route: first, permission from the Authorization

Committee, then from the Appropriations Committee, and in both cases there was usually testimony from a high official as to what use would be made of the money. Two billion was a lot of money even in Washington, and plenty of people would be asking why.

To tell why, Marshall explained, was impossible. It was a project that had to be kept in utmost secrecy. It had to be forthcoming right away for the defense of the country. Its future was at stake. The military needed help.

Without further questioning, Rayburn pledged himself to get it. He would stake his word, his personal integrity, his ability to get Congress to go along. McCormack agreed.

But McCormack, who worked every day to get out the votes on the House floor, knew it would not be too easy. Finally they did run into trouble in the Appropriations Committee, whereupon, at a subsequent meeting, Mc-Cormack recommended including the top men in on the secret.

The money was voted. Had it not been forthcoming, who knows what would have happened, for it was to be used for the Manhattan Project, the name given to the development of the atomic bomb.

The reason why Marshall said this was so urgent at that time was that the United States had obtained intelligence that Hitler was also building an A-bomb. If he won the race, he'd turn the bomb on this country.

McCormack, later to succeed Rayburn as Speaker, recalled the events vividly as he sat in his retirement office in Boston: "I believe that meeting was one of the most important conferences ever to be held in this country."

Rayburn was a man who could be tough as a goat. Or he could be touchingly tender if a member of his family was involved. He was devoted to his sisters, nieces, and nephews. A short, sad marriage brought little happiness and much silverware with their names on it, which his wife, who did not like Washington, took back to Amarillo, Texas, with her.

While Rayburn had immense power as Speaker, he was loath to use it for personal gain or even, at times, in fighting for his own district. He could use it in a minute for the nation, his first love. He despised people who said he loved power or that he was partisan and thought only about the Democratic party.

This gave me somewhat of a problem when I first started covering the office of the big man in 1946 for the *Sherman Democrat*. My publisher-editor, Frank Mayborn, told me that in my rounds as a reporter I should look out to make sure that the Pentagon did not close Perrin Air Force Base near Sherman, then a big source of revenue to the people who had not much else to go on. I didn't consider this lobbying. I was helping my paper work for its readers.

This from Mayborn, a man who had been almost clair-voyant in seeing the war coming and, before volunteering to go off to fight himself, had managed to get another giant industry, Fort Hood, for his hometown of Temple, Texas. (Fort Hood remains today the world's largest military training base, with a population of 50,000.)

I regularly checked the Pentagon on Perrin Air Force Base when budgets were announced, reorganization plans were laid, and appropriations sought. Was there to be more construction? Were units to be moved in or out? Gradually, the future for Perrin looked darker. Officials could not guarantee how long it would be open. After all, it was a training base. Were they planning to use it for any other purpose? The military doubted that appropriations could be passed in Congress the next year. I suddenly remarked in a meeting with officers at the Pentagon that I thought perhaps the bill would have no trouble passing; after all, the base was in the district of the Speaker of the House, Sam Rayburn.

That seemed to electrify them. They apparently had not connected the two before. They began to see how two and two made four and perhaps even more. I went back to the Capitol feeling lighthearted, and Perrin did stay open until 1971.

But I knew that I had said what Rayburn, who wanted the base to stay open as much as we did, would never have said himself. He was like that.

Often Rayburn would hear that some of the Texans who gathered daily in his outer office to win projects in Washington had said things in his name. At times they would be authorized to do so and at times not. One pipeline lobbyist, Thomas Corcoran, would appear at the Capitol when Rayburn would be eating breakfast in the restaurant, sit down, talk, and then report to clients later that day, "This morning, when I was having breakfast with Rayburn . . ." It was not always easy to get Rayburn to approve even a letter of application for a minor job. When he heard someone stepping outside the bounds of propriety, he would wrinkle his nose in disdain. I believe Sam Rayburn was strictly honest and strictly for the people of this country at all times.

Rayburn had absolutely no understanding of how to deal with the press. He never understood deadlines, or why the reporters who rushed him had such a sense of urgency. He was always utterly frank, but had a bad habit of telling us, "That's off the record." Whenever Rayburn appeared on radio and television, however, he would always say on the air what he didn't want us to print in the newspapers.

He could be very crude at times. If he did not like a man's position on politics, economics, social reform, or anything else, that man would get no help from Sam Rayburn. D. R. Strackbein, a Texas Republican and a sheep and wool man, was no friend of Rayburn's. He wrote the Speaker a letter demanding that Rayburn state his position on free trade versus tariffs, an issue important to Strackbein. Rayburn never answered the letter, and I thought there might be a story in it, so I asked Rayburn repeatedly about the Strackbein letter at a succession of the Speaker's press conferences.

One day, he finally said, "Sarah, here is my answer: 'Dear Mr. Strackbein, I have your letter before me—I now have your letter behind me—and I will pull the chain.' "

I blushed. Rayburn, who grew up in a rural community, was quite familiar with the old-fashioned chain-type toilet.

# 9

# My War for the Veterans

My long interest in the military, which really started when I worked on the *Beaumont Enterprise* and intensified during my years with the WACs, alerted me to a problem no one in government seemed to be aware of during the Nixon administration.

I first learned that the federal government was not dealing fairly with Vietnam veterans in the fall of 1973, when a staff member in the office of Congressman Richard D. White, Democrat of Texas, showed me a stack of letters from veterans going to school under the GI Bill in his district, which included El Paso. The veterans complained that checks promised them by the Veterans Administration arrived late—weeks and sometimes months behind schedule. When I started checking with other congressional offices, I found veterans all over the country were complaining about the same problem.

Veterans who tried to take advantage of what our government offered them soon found that they were being mistreated by the system. The government had agreed to send them to school under the GI Bill and send them monthly checks to pay for tuition, books, and living expenses while they were attending high school, vocational school, or college. But the checks were almost never sent out on time. I found that many veterans at the University of El Paso were having crucial problems paying their bills.

At that time, the White House was issuing presidential statements (there were two in December, 1973) that described how much the Nixon administration was doing for veterans. Statistics were cited showing how many veterans were going to school under the GI Bill, and the statements went on to say how hard the White House staff was working to keep the veterans satisfied. It was not difficult for me to imagine what kind of repercussions statements like that had on the veterans themselves. I actually felt embarrassed for Richard Nixon, who obviously believed what he had been told, which was not the truth. The veterans had big problems, and Richard Nixon was being told that they did not.

I began to ask more questions. For months, I asked questions at the Veterans Administration, the Washington headquarters of the various veterans' organizations, and in senators' and congressmen's offices. Public interest lawyers working for Ralph Nader gave me some real answers, especially when I wanted to contrast veterans' problems in the seventies with the problems of the veterans of World War II. And, of course, I spoke to the veterans and wrote stories about their plight.

I discovered that when the checks failed to arrive the results were disastrous. Hundreds of thousands of veterans were forced to borrow money to pay their grocery bills. The government had not paid their tuition directly, as was done after World War II, so the veteran's education itself was often in jeopardy. And because the checks that were to be used for books, living expenses, and the like were so late, some of these veterans and their families were facing eviction. I also learned that nearly every office on Capitol Hill had received numerous complaints, but a far larger number of veterans were suffering in silence. In fact, it was this silent majority that kept the president and even the VA from knowing how large the problem was.

Congressman Kika De La Garza of Texas, who had a mounting pile of complaints on his desk, told me that I had "tapped a very vital national problem." Alan Cranston, Democratic senator from California, told me the same thing in a letter of praise and encouragement. Cranston is on the Senate Veterans' Affairs Committee and is one of the most persistent legislators working on behalf of deserving veterans.

But my repeated inquiries to the White House, asking when the problem would be resolved, brought no response. As far as the president and his staff knew, there was no problem. Maybe there had been a problem once: I noticed a wire service item from San Clemente which said that the problem of late checks for veterans had been resolved. Donald Johnson, VA director, the story said, had personally gone out to the West Coast to work on it. That was wonderful news for veterans in California, I told Johnson at the White House Press Center, but what about the veterans in Texas, Pennsylvania, and New York? Johnson told me I didn't know what I was talking about, that the problem had been local, not national, and was under control.

I learned later that the matter had been brought to Johnson's attention by the White House, after a man who had known Nixon personally, a college administrator in Southern California, called Nixon's attention to the problems veterans were having on his campus. A White

House staffer who happened to be working on Saturday learned of this. From that point on, a mad effort was made to expedite the check payments to that part of the country. But this only happened in Southern California; nothing was done about helping veterans in the rest of the country.

On February 20, Ron Nessen, then a newsman for NBC, did a special report for his network on the plight of veterans at colleges in Maryland. Nessen also said that these conditions were duplicated on other college campuses throughout the country. I called NBC to offer my congratulations, which led John Chancellor to report erroneously that I became interested in this problem because of Nessen.

I was in New York City covering the settlement of an employees' strike at Farah, the El Paso slacks manufacturer, when I heard that Nixon would be holding one of his infrequent press conferences that evening. I canceled all my plans and hurried back to Washington, determined to take the veterans' question straight to the president once and for all. To me, the greatest advantage of the press conference was that a reporter could take an important question, a question that directly affected people's lives, to the president of the United States—and sometimes could even get an answer.

Back in Washington, in preparation for the press conference, I telephoned the Veterans Administration. Odell Vaughn, one of the VA's top officials, told me that he and Donald Johnson were checking on reports from all over the country. Mr. Vaughn, then chief of benefits, said he and Johnson held weekly conference calls with VA administrators nationwide to learn how many complaints each had received. Next, they would dip into the mail, fish out several samples, and take what they read as a barometer of the situation throughout the country. I was shocked and horrified that the VA, the third largest agency in government, would consider this out-of-a-hat sampling adequate research—especially when the livelihood of veterans was at stake.

I finally asked President Nixon about the delayed checks on February 25, 1974. At first, he verbally pushed me aside and rejected my question. But I insisted that he had been misinformed. The transcript reads like this:

McCLENDON: Mr. President, Sir, I want to ask you something. I know you are not . . .

NIXON: You have the loudest voice, you go right ahead.

McCLENDON: Good. Thank you, Sir. I don't think that you are fully informed about some of the things that are happening in the government in a domestic way. I am sure it is not your fault, but maybe the people that you have appointed to office aren't giving you the right information. For example, I have just discovered that the Veterans Administration has absolutely no means of telling precisely what is the national problem regarding the payment of checks to boys going to school under the GI Bill, and many a young man in this country is being disillusioned totally by his government these days because of the hardships being put upon him.

NIXON: Well, this is a question which you very properly bring to the attention of the nation. It is a question that has already been brought to my attention, I am sure, by a number of people. . . .

McCLENDON: But, Sir, you had Mr. . . .

NIXON: . . . and the question . . . if I may give the answer now . . . is very simply this. Mr. Don Johnson of the Veterans Administration, as you know, acted expeditiously when we had a case in California. We have another one in Illinois at the present time. There are a great number of veterans. We have an adequate program to deal with it, and I can assure you that when any matter is brought to my attention, or to his, we will deal with it as quickly as we can because our Vietnam veterans and all veterans deserve whatever the law provides for them, and I will see that they get it.

McCLENDON: He is the very man I am talking about who is not giving you the correct information. He stood up there at the White House the other day and gave us false information. He has no real system for getting at the statistics on this problem.

NIXON: Well, if he isn't listening to this program, I will report to him just what you said. (*Laughter*) He may have heard even though he wasn't listening to the program. (*Laughter*)

I was so glad to get his promise of a response that the sting of the ridicule and criticism of my asking was dulled. Besides, I knew from past experiences as a woman reporter and activist that I would get ridicule.

Reaction to my question—and to its follow-up—was immediate. I had opened the eyes of the president and the American public to the Pandora's box of multiple errors, injustices, delays, insensitivity, no-recourse decisions, and adverse rigidity that was the VA. My question and the veterans' problems came as no surprise to anyone who ever had to deal with the bureaucracy of the Veterans Administration.

My colleagues in the press were quick to say that I had misbehaved yet again. The *New York Times* wrote an unfavorable editorial about my question. They had previously criticized me in an editorial and in several news articles. Eric Sevareid, the commentator, said on the air that I had "given rudeness a new dimension" by the way I talked to President Nixon. That stung me, because I never intended to be rude. I was just determined to make the problem clear to Nixon, and when he treated my original question on veterans as if there were no real problem, I followed up on my own question, something I never even *thought* about doing at a White House press conference. Besides, I was being critical of the president's staff, not the president. I was completely convinced that he was being fed misleading information by the VA. Again and again during the Nixon administration, the White House did not really know what its own people were doing. In the end, this was a fatal flaw.

To his credit, President Nixon started dealing with the veterans' question within seconds after the press conference ended. Although it was after 9:30 at night, he told an aide to get Donald Johnson on the phone. The next day, at the White House, Nixon told Johnson to "get with Sarah," talk things over and straighten them out. He added that after we talked, he wanted Johnson to give him "chapter and verse." It was an important problem, since the Veterans Administration is the third largest agency of the federal government, and it affects about one half of the population either directly or indirectly. In addition to veterans, the VA deals with their dependents, their relatives, and the survivors of those killed in the war. The VA helps with sustenance, compensation, hospitalization, pensions, education, housing, and burial.

When I got home, my phone was ringing, too. Veterans of all wars, from all over the country, began shouting with joy over my telephone lines, expressing their thanks that someone had taken up their cause. And my mail was staggering. I received so much mail that it had to be brought from the post office by special truck in canvas sacks. It was hard to open and read all the letters, and answering them was impossible. The veterans all said that they didn't think anyone knew or cared about their problems. A Women's Army Corps member, by herself at an isolated post in Louisiana, said, "I got up and danced around the room with joy."

Donald Johnson called, too, but not until the late afternoon, just ten minutes before he scheduled a press conference. Although the conference was to be held clear across town, I was there for the first question.

For three months after the press conference, every time I would sit down at the typewriter to work, I would get a phone call with a new, sad story. When my telephone bills arrived, I discovered that as I returned their calls, I frequently ended up paying for the call under the telephone company's billing system. I ended up owing a telephone bill of several hundred dollars, which I could not afford to pay. About that time, I received a letter from an old friend of mine in Texas, who said, "Gal, you must be incurring considerable expense with all this—here is a check to help you take care of this." I was so grateful I knelt down and cried.

Each tragic report was worse than the previous one. Although these stories were certainly good news stories, they were all the same story: that of a man whose life was interrupted by war, who now needed his country's help, but who did not quite fit all the specific regulations of the VA. These regulations, after so many years, had the same restriction as the Bible on sin—they did not stretch or bend.

Although I knew the veterans were having terrible problems when I asked my question, I had no idea how far-reaching these troubles were. Nineteen percent were unemployed and were getting no real help from the Labor Department. The White House was constantly threatening to cut off many of the programs. Many men had received "bad" discharges, and were unable to get a job because of identifying symbols on their service records. Some of these men, unable to get their veterans' benefits, were doomed to lives of crime or to live as wards of society. Thousands who never finished high school did not know that their GI rights would pay them to get their diplomas. The medical program was a shambles also. Some veterans hospitals had 1,000 beds with no full-time chief of medicine or surgery and often not nearly enough medical treatment, with an insufficient number of attendants. This situation with regard to attendants was worse on weekends. It is said that the loneliest place in the world is a veterans hospital on weekends.

President Nixon's response was, as I said, quick and thorough. And on March 12, 1974, he made a radio address to the nation from Key Biscayne in which he mentioned me by name and called me a "spirited reporter." That phrase was chosen after careful thought by White House staffers, one told me later. He said I had asked a valid question. He also said that Donald Johnson was going to conduct a thorough study of all his agency's hospitals. That did not go over well, so a new chief of medicine, Dr. John Chase, was named to do the study. Soon it was announced that Donald Johnson was through at the VA. He asked to remain for a few weeks, then managed to stretch it out until late September, when he found a well-paid berth in the Commerce Department. I rode herd on Johnson's exit by calling the VA and checking every ten days.

I like to think that President Nixon and I both accomplished some good for veterans. Very few presidents would have admitted that they didn't know what was going on in one of their agencies. Few men at any time would have acknowledged on network radio that a White House reporter (me) had been right to bring up the question in the first place.

Although my fellow reporters had a rough time with Richard Nixon, he was extremely nice to me. Whenever he saw me, he grinned and waved. He once made a special effort to have H. R. Haldeman get me the exact dates of a trip he was planning to Texas so I could include them in my story ahead of others. Almost every time I appeared at the Oval Office with a group of reporters for a picture-taking session, he would smile at me and say something personal. A White House photographer once told me, "The president must like you; he mentions you by name more than any other reporter."

Once, when several of us were close to his desk at the end of a press conference, I told him how nice he looked and asked him if he was wearing a new suit. He looked very pleased, replied that the suit was new, and told me to feel the material. He held out his arm. Though I never thought of doing such a thing, I did not want to be rude, so I touched his sleeve. "Isn't it soft?" he asked. It was a new kind of material that had been made into a suit for him by a tailor from Philadelphia.

When Nixon sent Secretary of Agriculture Clifford Hardin to Texas to survey drought conditions, he told him to "be sure and take Sarah along." When Hardin told him the plane he was flying in was too small to take a reporter along, Nixon told him to take a larger plane. That way, other reporters got to go, too. It was a nice trip, and I got a good story out of it.

Nixon specifically requested that I be included on a trip he was making to Dallas, and gave me an exclusive interview in his private cabin on *Air Force One*. We talked so intensely, eyeball to eyeball, that we did not fasten our seat belts as we landed, which terrified me at the time. After all, a president's safety is pretty important. But so is an interview, and besides, Lyndon Johnson taught me never to interrupt a president.

Once, while attending a "photo opportunity" (a White House term for bringing in photographers and reporters to photograph and observe the president with dignitaries), Nixon interrupted a conversation in his office with King Faisal and Ambassador Ibrahim Al-Sowayel of Saudi Arabia, Defense Secretary Melvin Laird, and Secretary of State Henry Kissinger to ask me why I didn't travel more, either with him or with Mrs. Nixon. I explained that it cost money to travel, and since I had no major newspaper, wire service, or large news bureau behind me, I couldn't afford to travel much. (Nixon remembered that and was once kind and generous enough to arrange free transportation for me when he was going to Texas for the dedication of the Johnson Library in Austin. When I saw Lyndon Johnson that day, he seemed pleased that Nixon had brought me. Johnson had invited me, but on a pay-your-own-way basis like other guests who were not on the program.)

Nixon kept our conversation on travel economics going for such a long time that day when the Saudi king was there that I was beginning to feel quite embarrassed. Ambassador Al-Sowayel, whom I knew well because my daughter had been a member of his embassy staff, looked horrified that the president had turned from their conversation to talk to me. Later, I wondered if Nixon had been talking to me in order to avoid an unpleasant confrontation with the Saudis. I believed I served as a timely diversion for Richard Nixon. I learned that on this occasion, they wanted an agreement, and Nixon was not willing to compromise his relationship with the Israelis.

I really appreciated Nixon's thoughtfulness when I received a personal invitation to one of his famous, unique Sunday church services in the White House. Lucy Winchester, the Nixons' social secretary, said, "You know why you're a guest today, Sarah? The president himself put your name on the guest list."

I felt honored to be included in this service as a guest. When I attended the services in the past it was as a reporter. Reporters were allowed to put their names down to cover the event, subject to White House press office approval. Then they sat or stood in the back of the room and went into the State Dining Room for the reception afterward, but did not go through the receiving line to shake hands and be greeted by the President and Mrs. Nixon, as did the persons who were invited guests.

When I was a guest, I sat up front near the Nixon family. It was while there that I looked across at Julie Nixon Eisenhower, who was in the same row as myself. I had a good look and realized with a shock that her face had an expression of abject pain and deep sorrow. Something was seriously troubling this young woman, in her mind and soul. That was April. The president went out of office in August.

With a guest list like Nixon's, it wasn't hard to get stories. I'd just speak to people after they came off the receiving line. The variety was incredible. I met boxer Joe Frazier, Billy Graham, a Catholic cardinal, racing car driver Cale Yarborough, Richard Nixon's aunt, and a CBS technician, Toni Janak, who had long worked in New

York on presidential television. Although it was part of my job to meet the greats and near greats of the world of politics almost daily, who would have ever thought that I'd be talking to Joe Frazier and Cale Yarborough?

It was at one of President Nixon's prayer breakfasts that Spiro Agnew, then vice-president, apologized to me for using my name in the punch line of a joke he told to a convention of UPI editors. Hubert Humphrey had taken a new job as an airline steward, Agnew kiddingly told the editors, and though he liked the work, he was surprised when Sarah McClendon pinched his bottom. Agnew and his public relations man, Vic Gold, said they were sorry they used my name, but I was the only female reporter they could think of whose name was known by everybody. I'm sure I'm the only reporter Agnew ever apologized to in his life.

Nixon even showed flashes of humor when he spoke to me. It was very cold in Washington on the day the Chinese Ping-Pong team from Peking was scheduled to come to a reception in the State Dining Room of the White House. That morning, I put on a pantsuit, an outfit that I never thought would be particularly flattering for my figure, but it was warm. I meant to go home and change before going to the White House that afternoon, but I was too busy and ended up in the East Room dressed as I was when I started the day. Perhaps someone told the president that I was wearing pants, something new for female reporters at the White House.

I don't know, but it seemed odd to me that immediately after leaving the podium, he made his way through the crowd directly to me. He was leading Mrs. Nixon, and when they were a few feet from me, they stopped. The president stared at me from head to toe and motioned for his wife to look, too. At that point, I was looking for something or someone to stand behind. I wanted to disappear. Pointing a finger at me, Nixon said to his wife, "I thought she was a traditionalist." "Since all your guests are wearing pants today," I replied, "I wanted to make them feel at home." With that, he grinned broadly.

I saw Nixon's sense of humor in evidence again when he was leaving a press conference at which I had not been able to get in a question. As he passed by me on his way out of the room, I said to him, "Mr. President, you're getting gray." He went halfway down the aisle, stopped, and walked back to me to ask what I'd said. When I repeated my comment, he said, "That's not gray—that's streaking!" Everyone howled, and the photographers took dozens of pictures of Nixon and the press laughing together after what had been a rather dull press conference. Streaking was a popular campus fad at the time, but I didn't know Nixon had heard of it.

Nixon and the press did not usually have such a pleasant relationship. We were suspicious of each other's motives, often with good reason. Reporters often felt that the president was taking advantage of us, using the power of his office to gain exposure on network television when such exposure was not justified. Of course, Nixon was not the only president who was guilty of this. Once in a while, one of the networks would threaten not to broadcast one of the president's announcements, but they usually gave in, with much grumbling by that network's reporters. Situations like that made reporters feel they were merely backdrops on Nixon's stage.

Like the Johnsons and the Fords, the Nixons placed a high value on photographs. The "photo opportunity" invented by President Nixon was really just a tool for using the press, an occasion for photographers to take pictures of the president and his visitors. Reporters could attend, but only as silent observers. Since no questions could be asked, reporters tried to listen to the president's conversations in an effort to get a story. We watched the president's mood, his appearance, everything about him for clues on what to write. These photo opportunities were sometimes helpful for me, especially if I had some background information on Nixon's visitor. I once got a very important story out of one of these sessions when I overheard some black leaders thanking him for giving federal aid to research on sickle cell anemia for the first time.

No other reporters seemed to have heard of the disease. I knew something about it, but not much. I called a black man who was on Nixon's staff and he had never heard of the disease. When he and I both found out how large a part of our population is threatened by sickle cell anemia, we were both ashamed. No reporter at the White House wrote that story but me.

Nixon was usually ill at ease in the presence of reporters. Once, after a nationwide broadcast during the Watergate era, he ducked out of the Oval Office, hurried down a long porch along the side of the West Wing, and entered the press center through a side entrance. He went to the microphone and hastily mumbled some phrases reminiscent of the "You won't have Dick Nixon to kick around anymore" speech and added that he hoped someday we'd trust him. By the time I had set up my tape recorder, he was gone.

I can understand why Richard Nixon believes that he received harsher treatment from the press than any president before him. This is partly because reporters are so much better at their jobs than they used to be. They are better educated, more knowledgeable about how government really works, and even seem to have more nerve than in the old days. Once these young reporters saw how thinly covered up Nixon and Company's misdeeds really were, they tore into the Watergate story and never let go. Nixon, of course, tried to make the American public believe that reporters were out to get him and that he was the underdog. Many people believed him, too; even after the tapes were discovered, the press was still being blamed for running Nixon out of office.

During Nixon's last year in office, he whipped up so much public opinion against the press that I would not have been surprised to have seen a reporter tarred and feathered by Nixon supporters. I remember being in a group of reporters who were covering a luncheon just a few weeks before Nixon resigned. Rabbi Baruch Korff, the self-appointed defender of Nixon, was the main speaker. During Korff's speech, we were surrounded by angry Nixon loyalists, who denounced us for not copying down Korff's every word. It was an antagonistic crowd and I felt in personal danger. We should have received combat pay for that assignment. While working reporters were being tormented, columnists Victor Lasky and Nick Thimmesch were seated as guests up front.

One reporter who was on Nixon's side and thrived during the Nixon administration was Ken Clawson. During Nixon's early days in office, Ken started writing a lot of good stories with "inside" information. I discovered Clawson's source when I attended one of Attorney General John Mitchell's press conferences at the Department of Justice. Mitchell stuck his head out of a side door, looked over the throng, then refused to begin taking questions until Clawson, at that time a reporter for the *Washington Post,* was present. Ken had been writing what Mitchell thought were "fair" pieces about the Department of Justice. Mitchell trusted him. Mitchell was using Clawson, Clawson was using Mitchell, and I imagine the *Post* was happy to have one reporter whose stories sounded pro-administration.

The affinity between Mitchell and Clawson came out into the open when Clawson left the *Post* to go to work for the Nixon White House. His job was to arrange invitational press briefings in the building next to the White House. These were intimate little affairs. Liz O'Neill, a beautiful girl, would help pass out news releases, drinks, and snacks to the lucky reporters whom Clawson invited. The reporters present were aware that a pitch was being made, that they were only hearing one side of the story. But even though they knew that what they heard was the Nixon party line, the reporters felt they should report what they heard at these briefings as news or else see their competitors scoop them on the basis of inevitable leaks.

The Nixon administration added a researcher to the press staff who had the job of finding answers to reporters' questions that couldn't be answered at press conferences. I believe I helped create this job. I was told they had me in mind when they came up with the new policy because I asked so many questions that required follow-ups. The job went to John Carlson, who proved to be very good at it. Somehow he managed to get the facts, be truthful, and keep us all calm, himself included. He was one of the best things about the Nixon press operation, and he stayed at the White House to go on doing the same job for President Ford.

The Nixon staff did not actually know too much about government. Haldeman and Ziegler both had backgrounds

My colleagues on the *Tyler Courier-Times* came up with a cake for my birthday.

At my first office as a Washington news-paperwoman.

As a WAC public relations lieutenant in the World War II Pentagon.

Getting into the reporting swing in Washington.

Doug Chevalier, the *Washington Post*

Asking a tough question of President Nixon.

NEW MEMBER
SARAH
McCLENDON

Among the first group of women to be admitted to the National Press Club, I couldn't help shedding a tear or two.

If you took my phones away, I'd be out of business.

I still don't have a fancy office, but then I've never needed one.

Lady Bird could handle LBJ
and any reporter, including me.

I always thought Pat Nixon did a better job than she got credit for.

Hubert Humphrey came for a party given in my honor; we're with my daughter, Sally.

Reporting has taken me to many places, including the Strategic Air Command headquarters in Nebraska.

I've always liked former Senator George Murphy of California, the one-time movie star.

Reporting can be a muddy job: trudging after Defense Secretary Melvin Laird.

I fought for the veterans, and they've always liked me for it.

in public relations. Ziegler had helped make tourists happy at Disneyland. But they seemed to have a lot of enemies. I really had a hard time with John Ehrlichman during a persistent campaign of mine to do something about mental health centers for mentally retarded children. But each time I brought up the question, the other reporters grew restless, and nobody knew what I was talking about. I asked Ehrlichman about this at a White House press briefing, but instead of answering my question, he said, "Now, if you were to ask me if you had been to the beauty parlor lately, I would say no. . . ."

I was furious. True, my hair didn't look very good that day, but care for the mentally retarded seemed to me to be a more important subject. I knew he was referring to my hair to ridicule me and punish me for asking a hard question. Senator Bill Brock of Tennessee, a Republican and a friend of the administration, had received 3,000 letters about these kids, who were being done out of funds and opportunities by their government. Remedial training centers were being closed and the children were being sent home to face bare walls and to rock. Yet the White House knew nothing about it. Deputy Press Secretary Gerald Warren and John Carlson were trying to find some answers for me, but when they telephoned the Department of Health, Education and Welfare, they were told the problem didn't exist.

I told Warren that I had a taped interview on the subject of mental health centers with Representative Robin Beard, Republican of Tennessee. Parents complained about there being no future for their kids. Warren asked an official of HEW to listen to the tape. After hearing the terrible things the parents of these unfortunate children were saying, the official responded, "Oh, I know what she is talking about—day-care centers." Then the people who counted finally got busy. Along with HEW Secretary Casper Weinberger, the White House made some changes to help the mentally retarded children in Tennessee and in other states, too.

I was joyful and gratified that my questions actually helped someone, and I was delighted to place my stories on mental health centers in my Mission Accomplished file. But I was still furious with Ehrlichman. As I was leaving the White House a few hours after he commented on my hairstyle, I saw him and Henry Kissinger coming in the gate on their way back to work from lunch. Ehrlichman left Kissinger's side, walked over to me, kissed me on the cheek, and said, "I shouldn't have said that about your hair."

"I'm on my way to the beauty parlor right now," I replied.

# 10

---

# *I Liked Jerry Ford, But...*

When President Jerry Ford called on seven women at his first formal White House press conference, he set a new record and inspired me to think that a new day of equal rights was dawning for women reporters. Ford's performance at this press conference was excellent. His many years of experience in the House of Representatives enabled him to explain public works programs, veterans' benefits, and energy matters in a way so that the average citizen could understand and learn. Of all the men who have served as president of the United States, only Ford could match Lyndon Johnson's legislative background.

The first press conference was very important to Ford for his image and reputation around the world. People did not trust him. They wondered if he would be a continuation of Nixon or something new. Here's how it looked to an old aisle sitter.

Ford was relaxed and natural. His lack of television makeup was, to me, a sign that he intended to remain the same old Jerry Ford we had known in the House. As a reporter who has had her problems getting recognized, I loved the way he really seemed to call on questioners at random. It was not the same old two from the wire services, three from the networks that the rest of us had come to expect (and, in some cases, grown to tolerate) over the years. Ford moved around the room, calling on someone in back, on the side, in the middle, giving a chance to reporters who had been ignored, it seemed, during the entire Nixon administration. When Ford called on seven women, it was just one of the changes he had in store for us.

But some things stayed the same. Ford gave us as little access to his staff as Nixon had. We still had to go through Ron Nessen for most information. During the Nixon years, most reporters who tried to talk with a staff person were advised by the press office to talk to the press secretary instead. And if the reporter (me) tried again, her telephone calls were not returned. Some staff members ignored reporters' letters for months. Others ignored them forever. I can't say I blame the Nixon staffers, though. If they were seen talking to a reporter, they were held suspect by their superiors, and if a staffer ever joined a journalist for lunch, he would be blamed for any future stories written by that reporter. Though I tried for months, I was never able to get such an innocuous item as a list of staff members. Salaries were kept secret, and many staff names were never given out at all. A call to the White House switchboard to check on someone's title brought the response, "We don't give out titles."

It was no surprise that reporters were not treated well by Nixon's staff. After all, we were thought to be the enemy. But I was amazed when I found the tight security surrounding Nixon's White House extended to a senator from Nixon's own party. Senator Howard Baker of Tennessee walked out of the White House one day. I was waiting for him on the driveway to ask what he and the president had talked about. I began to ask him a few questions. As we stood and talked on the grass between the West Wing and the gate, a policeman came up and told us in no uncertain terms that we'd have to "move on."

"You can't talk here," he snarled.

"This man is a United States senator," I said, "and he can talk to anybody at any place he chooses." But the guard said we couldn't talk there.

"Sarah," said Baker, "how about getting in my car and letting my chauffeur drive us back to the Capitol." The senator was furious. On the ride to the hill, I got my story.

When Ford took the oath of office and moved into the White House, I could almost feel the entire country breathe a sigh of relief. Certainly the reporters felt more relaxed with Ford than they had with Nixon. It was a happy thought when Ford decided to get Jerald F. terHorst, who had long been a respected reporter for the *Detroit News*, to be his press secretary. From stories he had written, we all had the greatest belief in his integrity.

The appointment was decided upon, I am sure, to help break the distrust that many reporters held for the White House after the pallid no-answers and purposeful misguidings Ron Ziegler had been handing out. Poor Ron— he was told what to do by Nixon and Haldeman; it might have been better if they had taken his advice.

But terHorst's sense of integrity kept him from staying long as a White House press secretary. The actions there, involving scheming behind the scenes, secrecy, plotting, trading off promises, and compromising, were incompatible with his sense of forthright honesty. He resigned when he found out that President Ford had pardoned President Nixon when all the time he had been led to believe there would be no such action. It had been in the works all along.

Because I spent much of my time digging for stories and

doing research at the House of Representatives, I had known Jerry Ford for years. But I never thought he would become president, and neither did anyone else who knew him. In fact, when Speaker Sam Rayburn was running the House and later, when Carl Albert was Speaker, the reporters often made fun of Ford, a Republican leader who would never cause a ripple in the smooth waters between the two parties. As minority leader, Ford was following the examples of his predecessors, Joe Martin and Charles Halleck, who knew they were often powerless against the Democratic majority and the strong-willed Rayburn. They decided to be nice to Rayburn and, at times, cooperative. They knew there was no hope that the Republicans would ever control the House. They made a big show out of being partisan on the floor, but in their offices it was "good old Charlie," "good old Jerry," and a lot of mutual back patting between the Republican and Democratic leadership.

I was at the House of Representatives a few hours before Nixon named Ford as his new vice-president. In the Speaker's Lobby, a Republican reading clerk, Joe Bartlett, tried to convince me that Ford was Nixon's choice. I was incredulous. "Not him" was my answer. I expected it would be former Secretary of Defense Melvin Laird.

Although we had always gotten along well, there was the time when Ford was House minority leader and he turned me down cold when I asked him for funds, which he controlled from the Republican House Congressional Campaign Committee, so that I could run for Congress in my eastern Texas district. Senator John G. Tower, Republican from Texas, whom I covered regularly, also advised against it. Mary Brooks, later director of the mint but at that time assistant chairman of the Republican party, and some other southern Republican women urged me to become a candidate after I addressed the southern regional meeting of Republican women in Little Rock, Arkansas, on what I thought made a good congressman. I planned to run as a Republican against the conservative incumbent Democrat, Ray Roberts of McKinney. He voted with the Republicans most of the time. I wanted to bring the two-party system back to my traditionally Democratic district and, at the same time, add my vote to the liberal column in the House. Several highly influential Republican advisers in Washington had urged me to run. They thought that if I, a Democrat and a reporter who was well known, would join the Republican party and run on the ticket, this would give a shot in the arm to the unexciting party campaigns, especially in the Southwest. But Ford and party leaders had certain districts targeted to get the most of their scarce funds. They liked Roberts. He usually voted with them, and he and Ford were very good friends, I discovered.

I went back to Texas to look over the political situation. I was interviewed by local reporters who wrote flattering stories about me. State and district Republican leaders set up a meeting at the Petroleum Club in Dallas to talk to me about making the race. They wanted to know how many friends I had who would contribute anywhere from $1,000 to $10,000 toward my campaign. I was shocked. Being an independent woman, I decided I would not "sell my soul" for campaign contributions and make precommitments on votes. I returned to Washington to see if I could get campaign funds from the Republican National Committee.

Ford explained to me that the Republicans had their own preselected "targeted" candidates, as mentioned before. Any Republican running against Roberts, a Democrat who usually voted with the Republican administration, was not one of them, so I had to drop my campaign. Also, I learned Roberts's campaign manager and the area Republican chairman were law partners in Tyler. Looking back now, it was just as well. I think that the discipline of the House and of the party is something I would not want. I can do more as an independent reporter to change and improve government than I ever could as a member of the House of Representatives. I understood Ford's position and bore him no ill will because of this. In fact, I liked him personally.

I just could not see him as president.

A few months after Ford moved into the White House I was appearing on the "Good Day!" television show in Boston. The host, John Willis, asked me what I thought of Ford's qualifications for the job. I replied that although Ford was capable and a nice man, he was not presidential material. He did not face up to responsibility the way a president should. Instead of proposing change, Ford put most issues on a back burner until he was told what to do by an advisory board. A year later, when I was a guest again on the same program, they played back my old tape. "What do you think now?" Willis asked. "You know, it's surprising how right I was," I answered.

I never changed my mind. But Willis's mother told him she thought it wrong for anyone to criticize the president in public.

Yet President Ford became a real political animal in the job. When he ran for president in 1976, I realized I had underestimated his political ability. He desperately wanted to be elected president. He worked hard at it and came very close. But there was an ineptness in his campaign, as in his lack of leadership. It was as if he was waiting for too many other people to make decisions. Some never came.

Ford surprised me and most of the other reporters when

he became the scourge of Congress. After all his years in the House, one would have confidently expected that Ford, a product of the congressional career system, and Congress would have gotten along like twin brothers. In fact, I always thought that Nixon picked Ford because he wanted a man who would get along with Congress to serve as his vice-president. As president, though, Ford became such a critic, tormentor, and torturer of Congress that the public's opinion of both houses started to plummet. What's more, Ford became a manipulator of Congress. There were vetoes, threats of vetoes, Ford contact men breathing down the necks of congressmen.

Continuing my own little pursuit of trying to analyze the man in the White House, I decided that Ford, had he ever told all to a psychiatrist, would have said how frustrating it had been to serve all those years in the House without becoming Speaker—how he had wanted the job and how hard it had been for him to participate again and again in the selection of House Speaker and being nominated himself, knowing he had no chance. I think he would have said that it had been difficult to operate and to try to pass Republican bills with the Democratic leadership over the years. I think he would have said, "Now that I am president, I can finally be Speaker of the House, too. I am going to make up for all those years by driving those Democrats out of their seats, and out of their minds, if I can." And he almost did.

People often said—and I said it too—that Ford was the nicest guy to know personally, that he was easygoing, friendly, nice to his family, in love with his wife, kind, considerate, fun on the dance floor, and good on the golf course. They said that he had integrity, that he was honest. They also said that he was more of a football player than a statesman, that he was dull and possibly not up to the intellectual level of the heads of state he dealt with.

But just as he surprised us by taking the stump as a total candidate and by taking the whip to Congress, we found out that Ford could be a hard-liner too when it came to running his administration. He vetoed more bills than any other president. He whacked at budgets. He showed no compassion when he cut off or cut back federal programs.

As a congressman and even as minority leader, Ford had been shy and quiet, a Mr. Nice Guy who never made headlines. But once Ford became president, he showed himself to be anything but shy when it came to publicity. He actually began to try to manipulate the press, just as he tried to manipulate Congress, by creating an image of accomplishment. He spent hours of other people's time in his effort to make the public think a Ford program of substance existed. I can remember attending dozens of interviews and briefings in Washington (even more were conducted on the road) with the sole purpose of spreading the word about Ford accomplishment, Ford activity, and Ford success. Ford learned to be more skillful at public relations, especially when compared to the Nixon crew. He made special use of the public relations technique of "preventing" problems. If the Ford staff was contacted by a dissident group, they set up a meeting for the group with the president at the White House. He listened to them all: the Baltic nations, relatives of Vietnam MIA's, a group of farmers from Kansas who wanted to poison marauding western coyotes. He listened, he "recognized" their problems, and he promised that his staff would do a study. The word *study* usually meant nothing would be done.

One of Ford's most effective public relations tools was something new at the White House—the Office of Public

Liaison, created to get Ford out of his office and mixing with groups of people from many walks of life in America. Public liaison was an effective, unique, and original idea, directed by President Ford's public relations adviser, William Baroody. Baroody's family runs the American Enterprise Institute, an extremely well-financed conservative lobby representing business moguls with an interest in national security. He and his relatives have worked on Capitol Hill and at the White House for years.

Baroody scheduled hundreds of meetings with people from different ethnic backgrounds, income groups, regions, and interests, both at the White House and around the country. Baroody conducted many of these meetings himself. Others were conducted by Ford's staff or sometimes even Mrs. Ford. The president tried to get to as many of these meetings as he could, for he considered Baroody's efforts an important part of his campaign to be elected. To Ford, public liaison was as important as the press or Congress. These meetings gave Ford a wide exposure among people who had never come so close to a president before, and gave them a bond with him. They had a new and hopefully meaningful way to unleash their frustrations. They felt a part of the governmental process. They found the president and his staff personable and reasonable.

But Ford's public relations staff couldn't help him when it came to making decisions. It took Ford months to announce that an energy program would be sent to Congress. By the time it arrived on Capitol Hill, the winter was almost over. Yet Ford knew the situation had been critical. He seemed very hesitant to decide on a policy. I heard people say that Ford was indecisive because he was not elected. To me, this reasoning was unsound. I thought he was just incapable of leadership.

I can only think of two major decisions made by President Ford. The first was the Nixon pardon and the second was the *Mayaguez* incident. The pardon became Ford's biggest political liability, and while the *Mayaguez* action may have helped the president politically when it happened, more thoughtful analysis shows some of Ford's actions during that incident to have been questionable at best. I always wondered if a different action might have saved the lives of the approximately forty killed.

A careful look at the chronology of events relating to the Cambodian seizure of the merchant marine vessel *Mayaguez* shows that the president and the National Security Council made the decision to give the order for United States pilots to begin firing on Cambodian gunboats hours before there was any attempt to consult with key members of Congress. The decision was made before noon on May 13, 1975, but White House congressional liaison staff did not begin calling members of Congress until late that day. Before the series of phone calls to inform Congress was completed, the order was given to commence firing (at 8:12 P.M. Washington time).

The first boat was sunk at 8:30 P.M. Three gunboats were sunk in all, but one was allowed to escape unharmed because the pilots thought they saw Caucasian faces on deck. Earlier in the day the Cambodians had taken a number of American sailors prisoner off the *Mayaguez*.

By the time all the phone calls were made, it was midnight. I don't know what the White House staff had been instructed to say to the senators and congressmen. They certainly were never asked whether or not the United States should start shooting at Cambodians because the die was already cast before most of the conversations took place. And though the White House claimed the members

of Congress were consulted about this decision, Senator
Mike Mansfield, the Democratic majority leader who was
very knowledgeable about military matters in that part of
the world, told me he hadn't been consulted, only advised.
Mansfield said he expressed doubts all along, but to no
avail. Senate Assistant Majority Leader Robert Byrd of
West Virginia agreed with Mansfield. Representative
George Mahon of Lubbock, Texas, chairman of the House
Appropriations Committee and a highly experienced military expert, said that no one had asked him for any suggestions. When I asked him if he had been consulted, he
replied, " 'Consult' is a relative term."

I thought it was important to write stories on the
*Mayaguez* incident because I didn't want this action to
become a pattern for future government mishandling of
power. Ford chose to appear as if he were acting quickly
to save American lives, but the action produced far too
many casualties and the president's reasoning didn't stand
up. The record indicates that Ford, the National Security
Council, the Joint Chiefs of Staff, and the secretaries of
state and of defense acted without first consulting Congress,
as required by law in the War Powers Act. When key senators and congressmen were finally brought to the White
House, they complained bitterly and they kept complaining. The whole incident made me think of the time I'd
made Eisenhower so angry when I asked about sending the
marines into Lebanon. I didn't have to ask any questions
this time to make the public more aware of what went
wrong and how Ford could have done it right. The Senate
and many other reporters were asking those questions
for me.

The *Mayaguez* incident became a manipulation of the
press. It was designed to make Ford look good and capable

of quick, solid decisions as commander in chief. It blew out of proportion into a combat incident, which it need not have become. But what else could the Pentagon have done under his leadership? The quick decisions were front-page news—the casualty list came much later. It was unusual for the Pentagon to take long to count its dead.

# II

## Long-Odds Carter
## Takes Washington

Contacts can be a mighty important part in the life of anyone in public affairs. So it is with reporters. My father always told me that men who had met Woodrow Wilson at Democratic conventions later filled two of his cabinet posts. I often was guided by this fatherly hint on contacts.

So when my good friend, Malvina Stephenson, called to suggest that we go to Pinehurst, North Carolina, to attend a National Governors Conference seminar for governors newly elected in 1970, I decided this might be an interesting way to meet people. I really received dividends from that trip. For years I have written (and am continuing to write) stories about people we met in that group: Reubin Askew of Florida, whose roots really extended from eastern Texas and Oklahoma; Governor Dale Bumpers of Arkansas, later to be United States senator and possibly vice-president; Governor David Hall of Oklahoma, later to go to prison (for bribery and extortion); Governor Bruce King of New Mexico, who may get another term or be United States senator; Governor Robert Scott of North Carolina, whose wife entertained Malvina and me at luncheon; Governor Wendell Anderson of Minnesota, later to appoint himself to the United States Senate; and others. While there, I also taped radio interviews with a freshman governor and his wife—Governor and Mrs. Jimmy Carter of Georgia.

I recall that he was most impressive and quite serious. She spoke of herself as having a valuable part to play in his administration and said she planned to conduct a program to improve life for the mentally ill. She still believes that today, this time on a national basis. At the time, I remember being highly skeptical about what she could do, when she described her mental health project on my tape recorder. Later I learned she did it. Her project was a success. I realized that this soft-spoken little woman was an important political force and instigator of social reforms in any Carter undertaking.

I didn't talk to Jimmy Carter again until his formal announcement (on December 12, 1975, at the National Press Club) that he was running for president. It was an announcement that few took seriously. But I was so impressed by that speech—and by Jimmy Carter's ideas on public service and his experience as a naval officer, as a farmer, and as the governor who worked hard to reorganize state agencies and to create a system of zero-based budgeting—that I turned to my neighbors at the press club and said, "Why, this man should be president." I was impressed by the fact that he had tested ideas in governmental reform. He seemed to be a natural leader. My fellow newspaper reporters laughed at me as usual, and finally convinced me that Carter had "no chance." Oh, well, I thought, I guess I am too idealistic.

Although I was led to believe that Carter would never win the nomination, I followed his campaign closely and I consistently liked what I heard. When Carter repeated in speech after speech that the government had to become more responsive to the needs of the people, I realized that he was one of those rugged, cussed Southerners who didn't know when to quit and often dared to try, usually ending defeated. I doubted he would end up going all the way.

Carter's populist views reminded me of my father's ideas, of his neighbors' ideas, and of my own beliefs. I've never heard a really good definition of the word *populist*, but if the late Representative Wright Patman, former United States Senator Ralph Yarborough (both of eastern Texas), and Jimmy Carter are populists, so am I. I think that populism must spring from a respect for individual rights, a desire for better government and a higher standard of living for everyone.

During the campaign, I was often invited to appear in various cities on radio, television, and the lecture circuit. I was paid to give my analysis of Washington. I always described Gerald Ford as a nice, clean-cut, friendly man—the perfect next-door neighbor—but not the leader our country needed. They had asked for my view as an independent reporter. I had covered Ford almost daily at the White House, and, with the exception of the *Mayaguez* incident, I considered him overly cautious to the point of being anti-progress. I actually hurt for the country's sake when I heard him downgrade Congress, allowing United States citizens to lose confidence in their own government.

Listeners to a live Chicago TV broadcast called in to say I ought not to be so one-sided. On "Detroit A.M.," a TV staff person from the program rushed in at commercial time to say, "Please say something on the other side." But I had many requests to return.

But if I thought that an outspoken Carter supporter like me would receive cordial treatment at the hands of the

Carter press team at the Democratic National Convention in Madison Square Garden in New York, I was wrong. I didn't realize that the famous Carter "anti-Washington" bias included me. I found it was true, though, when I was part of a group of Washington-based reporters trying to cover the final meeting of the Georgia delegation. The meeting was a closed-door affair, and Jimmy Carter was to be the main speaker. But other press were seen going inside. As our group arrived at the door, we heard the whispered instructions: no Washington press. We argued, begged, pleaded, and demanded, but we were left outside when that door closed. Rex Granum, deputy press secretary during the campaign, stood guard. I watched as he let a few reporters into the room while he kept most of us out. One Washington newsman, Eugene Methvin of *Reader's Digest*, reverted to his native Georgian accent and was admitted immediately. "Only those with Georgia drivers' licenses," a security guard who had been instructed kept repeating to persons seeking to go in. That was too much for me. In my usual gentle manner, I asked if they would give me a blood test. After all, my ancestors came from Georgia.

At that point, Jimmy Carter walked up to the door, spotted me in the crowd, and came over and shook hands. For once, I kept my mouth shut and my problems to myself as I watched him go into the meeting room.

When I arrived at a convention press conference for Rosalynn Carter and Joan Mondale the next day, I was stopped and my three required press credentials were scrutinized by two guards. "How do I know your passes aren't stolen?" asked an unfriendly Carter security woman. They finally allowed me to attend the press conference when my fellow reporters protested this unfair treatment. After the

press conference ended, I went to Carter press headquarters.

"I am having a bit of trouble getting into things," I told one of the aides, "and I wonder if a special press badge that I don't have is required. If it is, I want it now, because I'll be covering you extensively in the future."

While my problem was being relayed to press aides Jody Powell or Rex Granum, I sat down to wait on a chair placed at the head of a flight of stairs. (I learned later that the Carter press office had placed this chair at the end of the small flight of steps and just outside of their press office to keep someone on watch about who was going in and out. The chair was empty when I found it. But why this feeling of need to keep watch anyway? I wish the chair had not been there.) It was a long wait. I had to tell my story several times. As I turned to greet a passing reporter, one leg of the chair slipped off the narrow top landing and I fell down six steps, head first. When I landed, the chair and my tape recorder landed on top of me. When I got up, my face was bloody and my neck out of joint.

With the help of Carter volunteer nurse Mary Myers of Brooklyn, I was taken by ambulance to the emergency room of St. Vincent's Hospital in downtown New York. Lying there, listening to the cries of the other patients, thought of Ruth Carter Stapleton, the candidate's si who said she could cure people's pains and sometimes their troubles with the power of prayer. I decided I try to use my own powers to try to quiet the wor to me, who was screaming in pain. I reached ove her hand in mine. She grabbed my hand gra quieted down.

Luckily, I had no broken bones and was a the hospital after I was X-rayed and clean I was too bloody and bruised to go back

Garden, so I watched Carter's acceptance speech on television in my hotel room. The whole experience proved to me that there is a powerful "Georgia Mafia" that surrounds Jimmy Carter and protects him from outsiders. This inner circle had already chosen favorite reporters by the time Carter won the nomination, men like Ed Bradley of CBS. The Carter story was much more important than the story of a reporter's access to the candidate, though, so I never wrote a story on the Georgia Mafia. I believed back then—and I still believe—that Carter can and will reorganize the government, and that he will develop a good working relationship with Congress.

"I am nobody's boss," Carter says, "I am everybody's servant." He brought hope to many Americans, including me, during a campaign breakfast in Washington for Democratic leaders from across the nation.

When Carter was elected president, he started working like a prairie fire, and there's no sign that he plans to let up. He spent his first days announcing the solutions to problems that had been swept under the rug by Gerald Ford, Lyndon Johnson, and John F. Kennedy. First, Carter dealt with the problems left over from the Vietnam War. He started one program to bring the boys home from Canada and Sweden, and another program to help Vietnam veterans find jobs. This would help both the veterans and the whole economy. Veterans of the Vietnam War had been mistreated for years—I made a splash with my question on the GI Bill in 1974—and Jimmy Carter faced right up to veterans' problems. Veterans were delighted when Carter named Max Cleland, a triple amputee from the Vietnam War, to head the Veterans Administration. I was one of he pool reporters who covered the swearing-in ceremony, d I was struck by Carter's sense of appropriateness. Sam

Brown, who led the national protest against the Vietnam War, was being sworn in at the same ceremony as head of ACTION. The contrast was striking between Brown and Cleland, who had already attained a master's degree but who felt it was his duty to fight and came home a triple amputee.

Then Carter moved on energy, the cold-weather crisis, and government reorganization. He strengthened the cabinet when he made each cabinet member autonomous, expected to run his (or her!) own shop with practically no guidance from the White House. I believe Carter's success is due in large part to the fact that he is so well organized. He has studied, has been briefed, is prepared, and it shows. I'm sure Carter learned about organization at the naval academy at Annapolis. I learned about it myself when I was in the WACs.

What I knew of Jimmy Carter's military experience impressed me more than anything else about him. Carter was handpicked by Admiral Hyman Rickover to be navigator on a nuclear submarine. Submariners are an elite group in the navy, and nuclear submarines were the admiral's special pets. Navy men told me that being screened by Rickover was a grueling experience, and that few men measured up to the admiral's high standards.

Carter's relations with the press have been excellent. Reporters have access to the White House staff, and we are allowed to question them directly. During the Nixon and Ford years, we were forced to go through Ziegler and Nessen, which could get pretty complicated. During Carter's first month in office, I called four of the members of his staff in one day and left messages for each of them to call me. All four of them called back, and each one helped with a story. Now that's an open administration.

Jimmy Carter holds regular and frequent press conferences, and he does a great job at them. His use of words is excellent, and his answers are well rounded and specific. He is very much in control of himself and the news conference. He seems to know beforehand who he is going to call on. After the first few press conferences, in which he fielded questions from all over the room, Carter returned to the old style of presidents taking two questions from the wires, three from the networks, and two from the Washington papers. He also calls on beautiful blonde Judy Woodruff, an NBC correspondent from Georgia.

He called on me at his very first presidential press conference. True to form, I asked him a controversial question.

McCLENDON: Sir, you have a man working on energy, Douglas G. Robinson. He was formerly deputy general counsel for the FEA (Federal Energy Administration). He works for Schlesinger and Dr. O'Leary.

CARTER: Yes, Ma'am.

McCLENDON: Congressman John Moss sent you some information down at Plains about information he had uncovered in Congress about the activities of this man in allegedly not enforcing pricing and protective regulations. Are you keeping him on knowingly, or you just didn't know about him?

CARTER: I didn't know about him, but I'll check on it after this press conference.

I never received my answer, although I was asked by Dr. James Schlesinger's office to submit backup material and I did, twice. Neither did the congressman get an answer to his letter from the President. President Carter was still not recognizing me at press conferences months later, although

I continued seeking recognition at every opportunity. Other reporters began to notice, and there have even been stories in the papers about it.

Immediately after the press conference, I was subjected to a steamroller of pressure from lawyers who worked with Robinson. They sought a retraction from me and a favorable story. I refused. My investigation of Robinson continues at this writing.

One case I investigated involved a city utility being overcharged for petroleum by a Houston oil company. This case was delayed by Robinson for nearly two years. He was trying to make it a civil case rather than a criminal case. Meanwhile, Robinson received a succession of temporary appointments in FEA and still sought an important permanent job. He had important people backing him. They very much wanted him to get a key job in the energy program.

Mine was the one question ABC lifted out of the press conference to show on its network news program. Some of the reporters liked my question; after all, it revealed a congressional investigation of a federal employee. But, as usual, I had many critics. "She named names," they said, and "She put a black mark against Robinson." One reporter wrote that I had once slandered a government employee at a Kennedy press conference, so no one should be surprised that I had done it again. The *New York Times* and the *Washington Post* attacked me for wrongly accusing a fine man in public. Even the *New Republic*, whose T.R.B. once wrote that I had "changed history," published a nasty piece by John Osborne, saying that my only national outlet was the president's press conferences.

This is hardly the case, as I now write for newspapers in Texas and Wisconsin, and do radio broadcasts every day for three stations in Tennessee, two in Georgia, and one in the Washington-Virginia area. I also write my own newsletter, and when I can, I write for NANA and for the tabloid *Midnight.* I am a regular guest on such television shows as "A.M. Chicago" and "Good Day!" in Boston and Detroit and other cities, and I give frequent lectures.

I asked Carter about Robinson because I believe a reporter can inform a president and tell him something he's never heard about. Some reporters can see the value of it; others never do. A reporter has the right to question the record of a bureaucrat who works in government and whose salary is paid by the people. If Congress looks at his record and finds fault, I can talk about that, even on network television. I never mean to create scandal, but if no one else is asking about something that needs to be asked, I will.

The Robinson story is about an official in the government bureaucracy who was lobbying for a top job in the Carter energy administration. Robinson may be the cleanest man in Washington, and his allies in government often say he is a "fine public servant" and a "good regulator." His detractors often express puzzlement about his strong motives in pushing so hard for a top job in energy. Anyway, he is a bureaucrat who is on the public payroll, and therefore I think the public is entitled to know more about him. How will Douglas Robinson affect the life of my readers? Will he cost them money? This kind of story is hard to present to the American people under the constraints of conventional journalism.

# I 2

---

# On the Record
# with J. Edgar Hoover

I have encountered the same journalistic constraints ever
since I went to work for the *Tyler Courier-Times*. In small
towns like Tyler, more news is kept out of the papers at
times by conservative editors than actually appears. "The
boss just told us not to print that," the editors used to tell
me, and it seemed that half the people in town had enough
influence to pull a story. Editors have a limited idea of what
is news. Most editors believe the news is what the wire
services write. Editors often don't want scoops. I've had to
educate some of my editors by explaining why I should be
the only reporter to be writing a story. The Bobby Baker
story is a perfect example of a scoop nobody wanted. My
own editors turned it down, and so did most syndicate
editors.

On the other hand, if I write on the same subject the wire
services cover, the editors are very reluctant to print my
story. But my story never merely duplicates what the wire
services write. A wire service story must be general, must
give the facts and little else. In the best journalistic tradition, the wire service story must tell the reader who, what,
when, and where. The now defunct International News

Service (INS) used to have a rule that all the facts of a story must be put in the first twenty-five words. These stories are well written, with excellent leads. In fact, many reporters wait to see the lead on the wire service story before writing their own leads, a custom that their editors heartily endorse. Editors are reluctant to trust a reporter who doesn't agree with what the wire service reporter wrote. But the language in these wire service stories is often skeletonized, patterned, abstract, and colorless.

My stories are different. My language is simple and direct, not the standardized prose the wire services churn out. Since I can't duplicate the wire service stories, I pick up on some angle of the story that will interest my readers specifically. I try to write the human side of the story. If I write a general story first, I'll then try to explain how it will affect my readers. "The attorney general announced that he would recommend a raise for border guards on the Texas-Mexico border" would be a good lead for me. My reader in Texas knows exactly what I'm writing about in this story, and knows what effect it would have on his life (or his neighbor's or cousin's paycheck).

I look on my readers the way a congressman looks on his constituents. I call them "my people" and, at times, I've fought hard for them. I worked for the people of El Paso for over thirty years. El Paso, isolated from other cities, yet not rural, had very special problems. I championed the rights of its citizens in offices on Capitol Hill and in my newspaper stories. I felt I was part of their developing economy. I was always watching for settlement of another conflict with Mexico, or whether the federal government would close down or reopen another international bridge, whether the college should get a new grant or the city a new industry. I thought I could really help by keeping the people

of El Paso posted on any upcoming federal expansions so
they could have part of the action.

Much of what would happen in El Paso was determined
in Washington. A reporter, in a sense, is a liaison between
the people and the government. Often a reporter must tell
a congressman what's happening in order to get his reaction for a story. People need to know how their congressmen react to certain problems and to get their ideas on
how to solve them, but first a congressman must be aware
of the needs. I've educated many a freshman congressman
who was too busy with his work on the hill to know when
something important was coming up in the departments or
agencies. Then he pushed for it. I got his reactions and a
follow-up. It's a question of exchanging information.

I think it is more interesting to see a story developed
from all angles than just to write a two-inch announcement.
I get more deeply into issues. I get involved with people.
When a delegation arrives in Washington from the grass
roots, I meet with them and learn the specific problems. I
try to find out what their congressman is actually *doing* to
help, not what he thinks about the pros and cons of the
issue. I'd rather write about people than about abstract
issues.

And I'd rather ask specific questions, naming names, than
ask the usual abstract questions so many reporters are
willing to settle for. Perhaps these reporters are just obey-
ing their editors. Since I'm independent, I choose my own
questions, and the questions I've come up with are not
what people are used to or have come to expect. It also
helps that I've lived in some of the communities for which
I still write. One night, President Nixon told a group of
reporters, "Sarah McClendon asks questions most men
don't have the nerve to ask," and he was right.

The men themselves are first to admit it. "Sarah, I wish I could get into the confrontations you get into, but the AP won't let me," a veteran reporter once told me, and I believed him. Some reporters are so worried about their images and about the opinions of their editors that they won't get up at a press conference and ask a question at all. That's a shame, because the more reporters we hear from and the more varied their questions, the better chance a reporter has of walking away from a press conference with a story.

I try to make my questions specific, and I like to get a specific answer. I don't believe in shying away from the facts. If I know something is true, I'm not afraid to talk about it, to name names, no matter whom it embarrasses, including me. If we don't face up to our problems, they will continue from administration to administration.

My outspoken questions have caused me to lose some jobs, and kept me from getting others. Editors tend to shy away from a reporter with my kind of notoriety. In Washington, when I attended a diplomatic function recently, I was introduced to several ambassadors as "Sarah McClendon, who asks the presidents 'those' questions." "Keep it up," most of them told me. But recently one of my editors told me, "Don't demand information in your usual way—get this story quietly." My reputation as a trouble-maker has hurt me more than it has helped.

Writing for small papers also has hurt my career. Although the total number of my readers (and now my television and radio audience) surpasses the circulation figures of some one-paper reporters with more "clout," I was the sole connection most of my papers had. I didn't write for a chain, or exclusively for a syndicate, for a single, easily identifiable audience, so the myth was perpetuated that I had few readers. But I liked my job and found something interesting in working for all my newspapers, whether it was writing a story about shrimp fishing in the Gulf, or snooping on an international secret conference of Prince Bernhard of the Netherlands and pals in Vermont, or a scandal in the navy at Annapolis.

I could have had more influence in Washington, but although I was trained in public relations, I never pushed myself the way some other reporters did. I also didn't have some of their advantages. Take the case of Nancy Dickerson, for instance. It upset me to watch Nancy entertain beautifully—political entertaining seems to be an occupational disease of journalists who can afford it— and using her social contacts to get stories.

I never had anyone working both sides of the street for me, and I felt that loss keenly. I didn't have anyone who was "selling" me, the way LBJ "sold" Marianne Means's column to uncommitted editors.

But both Nancy Dickerson and Marianne Means worked hard and were good reporters. I like to see any woman become a successful journalist, because there are so many obstacles all women have to overcome in this profession, no matter how much outside support they have. Editors are not anxious to pay women as well as they pay men. Many editors don't even like to hire women. I started running my own news bureau because Bascom Timmons had to give jobs back to the men returning from World War II. And if women do get hired, they usually get lesser assignments than their male counterparts. Editors try to limit women to writing "women's news," which is usually toward the bottom of any scale of importance. The easier, juicier assignments have traditionally gone to men. Most networks and bureaus assign a man to cover the White House and a woman to cover the president's wife. But neither the reporters, the editors, nor the readers believe that the First Lady's schedule is as important as the SALT talks.

Women reporters are treated differently from their male counterparts by their own readers. I get invitations all the time to speak to local groups. "Would you come speak to our Rotary Club?" I was asked by some of my readers from Sherman, who went on to suggest that I stick to "anecdotes about the presidents" in my speech. In other words, they don't want a woman's opinions and analysis—just the anecdotes. Can you imagine asking James Reston for anecdotes? That approach always amuses me as much as it disgusts me, because I always have a question-and-answer session after I tell the anecdotes, and my audience always gets to hear my eyewitness experiences and my analysis of what is happening. They seem to like the accounts.

Women reporters have a difficult time negotiating terms of employment. Most work with only a verbal agreement, broken easily at will of the employers. This shocked my attorney, Cathy Douglas, wife of retired Supreme Court Justice William O. Douglas.

I sought Cathy out as my attorney because I knew that she had a deep interest in seeing that women got equal justice under law. Also, she is an expert on retirement law.

Actually, women are still second-class citizens and will continue to be until the Equal Rights Amendment to the Constitution is adopted, I feel. That would be the overall blanket that would give equal justice to many men who hurt from discrimination in some instances as well as women. Under the amendment, sex would be left out of the application of laws.

When I went to Cathy, I had a case of great injustice, I thought, involving the *El Paso Times*. The *El Paso Times's* editor, W. J. Hooten, hired me in 1946 by telegram after he had been scooped by a rival paper with a Washington reporter. I worked for the *Times* for thirty years. At times there was hot competition between the *Times* and the *Herald-Post*, a Scripps-Howard newspaper, and through a succession of years the congressional races for that district were largely fought out in the two newspapers between Marshal McNeill of Scripps-Howard and myself. One time I'd win; next time he'd win.

After I had been working for the *Times* for about twenty years, I asked the publisher, Dorrance Roderick, to cut me in on the newspaper's retirement plan. I had learned that some of the staff, who had not worked as long as I, had received substantial benefits. He asked my age. I said fifty-five. He said he would have his lawyer look into it. The attorney said that I, being that old, would cost the paper too much. I was never admitted to the system.

Then Roderick became fearful that his heirs, including my former Washington intern, Francie Barnard Woodward, wife of the famed Watergate reporter, would be "too liberal" when they acquired the *Times*. So Roderick sold the paper to Gannett newspapers. They kept me on for several years because El Paso had special problems to solve in Washington and I was experienced. But in 1976 I was still left without a pension. In what may become a landmark case, I sued. Like other cases, it is being drawn out and is still pending. It is truly a woman's issue.

It is now much easier for women reporters, and the women who've come along in the last few years don't realize what we were up against a few years ago. These days, I see stories written by women in the financial section of the newspaper, the sports section, even the front page—parts of the paper once reserved for men only. But when I hear Sally Quinn of the *Washington Post* say that she's never been discriminated against, I want to tell about some of the women who paved the way. I was horrified when Sally announced in a speech to journalists that she thought sex entered into women reporters' getting a story now and then. In my journalism training, and my inclination, I shunned the thought.

I guess any woman reporter in Washington has been invited to a hotel room at night by a man using "I have a story for you" as bait. But I have never used sex as a come-on to get information. I believe that by far the majority of women reporters I know would never think of using sex to get a story. When I was invited to travel with Richard Nixon, it wasn't because of my sex appeal. When I was sitting on an airplane late at night, gossiping with Jack Kennedy and Lyndon Johnson, I wasn't under the impression that my charms got me on board. I was there as a reporter, I had a job to do, and they recognized this.

Women reporters, even Sally Quinn, have been excluded from some press events simply because they are female. We have to keep reminding the White House staff that women reporters exist, too. The staff has been known to set up special working dinners for heads of state that were stag affairs, and thus even pool reporters were confined to men only. At times, presidents and numerous organizations and officials have arranged events with correspondents at which they did not include one woman on the guest list. For years I picketed those stag parties they held at the exclusive Gridiron Club, where journalists roast government officials. All reporters, men and women, need access in order to write a story. It was not until the 1970s that the first woman was admitted as a member to the Gridiron Club.

It was because of this problem of access for women that I founded my press briefing group in 1963. I had come to realize that only a few women ever asked questions at press conferences I attended. Because they were only assigned to cover "women's news," many female reporters have never even met the men who really run the government. I wanted to create situations for more women reporters to have access to these men, and have a chance to write an important story for a change. I thought that if a group of women could hold informal, relaxed sessions, perhaps more of us could get to know top government officials and fewer of us would be shy about asking them questions.

Unlike other groups meeting around Washington, we put everything that was said at one of our sessions on the record. That was our only rule. We met for one hour, and any woman working in media in and around Washington could join. We integrated a few years later, so now men came to the meetings, too. I have only a small charge to cover the cost of sending out notices. We hold our meetings in the office of our "victim."

In the fall of 1964, I asked J. Edgar Hoover to schedule a press conference for my press briefing group. I had been trying to get Hoover to say yes for weeks, but I could never get the FBI's public relations specialists to actually name the time and the day. In one last attempt, I called them and said that if they refused to schedule a press conference I simply would never give them another opportunity. This was it. I nearly dropped the phone when they told me we could meet with Hoover on November 18.

I found out later that my press conference was the first press conference Hoover ever held in Washington, and the first anywhere with women reporters.

The J. Edgard Hoover interview was in many ways my briefing group's finest moment. The interview itself went on for almost three hours. Eighteen of us sat around a big table in a conference room in Hoover's large suite of offices. Agents plied us with coffee throughout. And the reporters who were present came away with a headline story, because it was at my press conference that J. Edgar Hoover publicly called Martin Luther King, Jr., a liar.

Hoover seemed glad to have an audience. He showed us the bureau's last annual report, proudly pointing out different portions of the text as if he didn't often get the chance to show it off. He also told us several things that were as interesting to me as his comments on King. He said that the Warren Commission report was "beyond a doubt the greatest example of Monday morning quarterbacking I've ever seen." He discussed the FBI's files on Lee Harvey Oswald, and called the Secret Service one of the most understaffed agencies in government.

Then Hoover started talking about the struggle for civil rights for blacks in the South. Hoover said that President Lyndon Johnson had sent him personally to Mississippi to see if he could find some means of working with the local law enforcement officers. While he was in Mississippi, Governor Paul Johnson told Hoover that he had been the first person from Washington who had ever spoken to him courteously. After that, Hoover said he got the greatest cooperation from Governor Johnson and the highway patrol. Hoover was having a harder time convincing local sheriffs to see things his way, but he thought the situation in the South was "improving." And then Hoover said: "Martin Luther King is a liar when he says the FBI is not making every effort to enforce the law in the South."

A short while before Hoover met with us, King was reported in the press as having told a group of black people in Albany, Georgia, not to give the FBI any information, and had warned them not to cooperate with its agents. Hoover felt it was wrong of King, and of other civil rights leaders, to expect the FBI to give protection to freedom fighters and civil rights workers in the South. He explained that the FBI's function is to investigate facts. The bureau protected no one, white or black. "We simply cannot wet-nurse anyone who goes down to reform or educate the South," said Hoover. As for King's allegations about the FBI, Hoover said that he could "prove that King is the most notorious liar in the country."

King was wrong, for instance, when he said that the FBI employed no blacks. The FBI had, at that time, twenty-five black agents and a total of three hundred black employees. "They say that all our agents in the South are southern boys," said Hoover, "so I checked and found that out of five agents in one southern area, four came from New York, Massachusetts, and Maine, and that only one was from the South. Seventy percent of all our agents were born in the North."

When Hoover finally stopped talking, our group split up and went to write our stories. The big news—the fact that Hoover had called King a liar—leaked out almost immediately. Within hours, papers from all over the country were calling. What else did Hoover really say, the editors wanted to know. Where could they get a transcript? The *New York Post* called me at six the next morning for the inside story. I wonder if they thought I'd be more talkative at that hour. Did Hoover realize that what he was saying was on the record? I told the *Post* the same thing I told the other papers and the same thing I told J. Edgar Hoover—with my press briefing group, everything is on the record.

Not all of our members came out of the press conference with a big story. One woman didn't think Hoover's remarks were very newsworthy and filed a skimpy story. Her editors thought the story deserved better treatment, and she lost her job. Miriam Ottenberg, who covered the Justice Department and wrote crime stories for the *Evening Star*, had not answered the invitation I had sent her months before to join our group, so she was not there. After the interview, she had to explain to her editor why she got scooped.

Our briefing group had previously been pressing Dr. King for a press conference. Now we wanted to hear his side of the story. But King didn't wait to meet with us. After Hoover's explosive statement appeared on front pages everywhere, King issued a reply the next day: "I cannot conceive of Mr. Hoover making a statement like this without being under extreme pressure. He has apparently faltered under the awesome burden, complexities, and responsibilities of his office. Therefore, I cannot engage in public debate with him. I have nothing but sympathy for this man who has served his country so well."

Then, according to *U.S. News and World Report* of November 3, 1964, he sent the following telegram to Hoover: "I was appalled and surprised at your reported statement maligning my integrity. What motivated such an irresponsible accusation is a mystery to me. I have sincerely questioned the effectiveness of the FBI in racial incidents, particularly where bombings and brutalities against Negroes are at issue, but I have never attributed this merely to the presence of Southerners in the FBI."

The Hoover-King battle was a good story, and because of it, the story of my press briefing group made the newspapers, too. I got special coverage as I was the first journalist to convince Hoover to speak to the press. Of course, not all my reviews were raves. Pat Saltonstall wrote for NANA that the "needler" of President Kennedy decided that "Mr. Hoover would be fair game for her press briefing group."

The *Pittsburgh Press* ran the headline "JFK 'Needler' Set Up Hoover." Some reporters asked why Hoover's remarks weren't put off the record. Of course, our group's only rule forbids off-the-record remarks. Had we been willing to listen to off-the-record comments, I'm sure J. Edgar Hoover would have had even more to say that day.

My standard reply to the on- or off-the-record question is that a reporter should be the last person in the world to turn down a usable story. When a man will say something for the record, I am not going to ask him to put it off the record so that I can't use it.

I got phone calls on the press conference for weeks. Some callers expressed shock; others praise. Some people even suggested that Hoover "used" the press briefing group as a means of getting something off his chest. Nothing could have been further from the truth. The FBI recorded the many telephone calls I made to them over the weeks it took to set up the meeting, and the comment Hoover made about King was in response to unrehearsed, unprepared, unexpected questions. It came apparently spontaneously, during his reading of a regular FBI report out loud, a report which was an afterthought with him and that he thought had not had sufficient coverage in the press.

To me, the most important aspect of the incident was that there were still, in the heyday of managed news that characterized the sixties, officials in Washington who would tell the public what they were doing and how they felt—if they were asked. More important, these officials would tell it on the record. What's wrong with that? The sad thing is that sometimes the officials go uncovered. Maybe no one asks them. That is why I always say there are millions of good, uncovered stories in Washington every year. We need more qualified reporters to get at these.

# 13

# My War with
# Secrecy in Government

If they have done nothing else, my years in Washington have given me an insight into the desperate public need for straight talk and solid information about the real operations of the people who run our government. If this awareness could have been achieved, the abuses of power that I have seen in Washington over the past thirty years—some of which I have helped in my own small way to expose or at least question—might have been eliminated. The Federal Bureau of Investigation's spying and other illegal activities against United States citizens (often covered up by fearful politicians), improper United States Information Agency activities abroad, the well-known Central Intelligence Agency abuses, and, of course, Watergate itself were all the result of misused power unchecked by public awareness. Perhaps with our post-Watergate consciousness, the rampant government secrecy that led to these excesses can be checked or eliminated. Congress has done a lot to open the doors with new legislation.

My own belief in the FBI as a bulwark of government was considerably shaken when *Redbook* magazine asked Cissy Farenthold of Texas, a national leader in the women's movement, to make up a list of suitable women who were qualified to serve as cabinet members and directors of key government agencies. She chose me to head the FBI in her mock administration.

I decided to do some research on my imaginary new job. First, I tried to locate the law that created and defined the FBI. I found that there is no one law which outlines or restricts the duties of the Federal Bureau of Investigation. When I asked people at the bureau about this, they hemmed, hawed, stuttered, and cited recent laws that were extensions of old laws. I finally learned that the FBI was established in 1908 by an executive order of President Theodore (Teddy) Roosevelt. Since that time, several laws have been passed that increased the power of the bureau slightly. Several laws have been passed to say what it could not do. The Lindbergh kidnapping law was passed, making kidnapping a federal offense and putting it under the enforcement of the FBI.

As I read and studied everything I could find about the FBI, I began to realize that this agency simply has too much to do. The FBI deals with espionage, sabotage, extortion, kidnapping, bank robbery, interstate transportation of stolen property, interstate gambling violations, fraud against the government, assault on a president or federal officer, unlawful flight to avoid prosecution, police academy training, and international police training. As if all that were not enough, the FBI investigates applicants for civil service jobs and federal appointments all the way up to candidates for cabinet posts, judgeships, and agency directorships.

The FBI has jurisdiction over six or seven million names in its files. Obviously, not all of the people represented by files can be criminals. In fact, the FBI encouraged civilians to place their fingerprints on file to help with identification in case of accidents, disasters, or amnesia. I filed my own prints with the bureau years ago. Still, the FBI is far too involved with the lives of average citizens.

The FBI has too much to do to be able to do any of it well. I believe that the FBI needs genuine reform. We clearly need a new law that spells out just what the FBI can and cannot do. This kind of definition would help to keep our country's major law enforcement agency on the right side of the law.

I was made even more aware of the need for closer supervision of the FBI after federal agents broke into the apartment of two young women in Alexandria, Virginia, one night looking for Patty Hearst. The agents broke the door in, claiming there was "no room" to slip their identity cards under the door beforehand. They did not have a warrant. Clarence Kelley, Hoover's successor as director of the FBI, said an investigation showed the agents were justified in their methods.

I tried at several White House briefings to get reaction on the civil rights angle, but President Ford backed Kelley. Subsequently, though, facts showed that the tip which led to this break-in was casual and farfetched. The FBI was no closer to Patty Hearst than before, and the one young woman who was home when the FBI broke in may never recover from the shock, physically and mentally. She will certainly never trust the FBI again.

So my high regard for the FBI began to fade. I had watched the FBI carefully for years, especially during the ten years when I covered the federal courts in Texas. I always felt that the agents were there for my own personal safety and that of all people. But I began to really doubt them when I saw how they controlled the late Martha

Mitchell when her husband was attorney general. She was watched, guarded, kept from talking to anyone, often prevented from keeping appointments. I know, because one of those appointments was with me. She had a highly authoritative bodyguard who questioned her appointments. She had one appointment with me and never showed up. Later, when I spoke to her about this when we met in person, she seemed to have no knowledge of having broken the appointment.

When I was more innocent about the FBI, I personally asked them for help at least three times. I had no hesitation about calling the FBI one night when a friend, Edith Kermit Roosevelt, granddaughter of President Theodore Roosevelt, called me to say that she thought her former husband, a one-time Soviet defector, was being followed by foreign agents. He felt that his life was in danger, and she was afraid that he would commit suicide. I told Edith to call the FBI. When she was too frightened to do so, I called for her and referred an agent to talk to her. I never heard more from the FBI. It is their custom not to tell persons outside the bureau what happened. I did hear that my friend's husband got safely to a hospital that night.

I called a second time when my daughter, Sally, who was then working at the Saudi Arabian Embassy, told me late one night about two terrorists who had come into the embassy that day, put a knife to the throat of one of the Saudi diplomats, and demanded two million dollars to establish a new homeland for blacks in Africa. I knew the Saudis would be too fearful of terrorist repercussions to report the incident to police. Sally had waited to tell me, knowing I would erupt, which I did. I had a personal stake in the situation—I wanted my daughter to be safe at work in the future—so I called the FBI to report what had happened and asked them to investigate the matter. I never heard more, but I was glad later to see the executive protective service created to protect embassies.

My third call to the FBI was made from Texas, where I heard a foreign businessman with important credentials say that he had seen Patty Hearst in Latin America on her way to Panama. I immediately phoned in the tip. The FBI came at once to interview me and him. Later, in San Francisco, I met the agent who had been in charge of the Hearst case as I was going into a television broadcast. "Say, that tip you gave us looked good—for a while," Charles Bates told me.

But when I discovered that the FBI had been used as a political weapon by Presidents Johnson and Nixon, I began to understand why Bobby Kennedy was so distrustful of it when he served as attorney general. None of this prepared me, though, for the stories about the FBI's twenty-four-hour surveillance of Martin Luther King, Jr., for the way the bureau threatened and harassed him, or for Kelley's admission (when he knew he was about to be exposed by the Senate Select Committee investigating the FBI and the CIA) that the FBI had illegally burglarized many a private home in the United States, and had even broken into foreign embassies.

The day of Kelley's admission, I attended a White House press briefing. When the subject of the FBI came up, Press Secretary Ron Nessen maintained an offended attitude of guarded isolation, so typical of the White House at times. Nessen was all innocent disbelief. Burglaries? The FBI? Who said that? "I didn't know . . . ," said Ron, innocently. When I'd had enough of Nessen's ivory-tower attitude, I interrupted to tell him that Kelley had confirmed the story himself. What further proof did Nessen need?

Nessen still refused to comment on the fact that a federal law enforcement agency had obviously been violating the law. I asked Nessen to give us a copy of a memorandum that President Ford had reportedly given to Clarence Kelley shortly after he became president. The memo directed the bureau to continue to carry out surveillance on citizens of the United States if it was being done in the name of national security.

"I do not know whether or not I can get that" was Nessen's answer, as usual. I never did find out who would define or limit the phrase "national security." Our recent, bitter experiences have shown that errors in judgment do occur, and that some men assume and use power in the wrong ways. The CIA, the FBI, the IRS, and the defense intelligence agencies have all been guilty of spying on United States citizens. And the United States Information Agency has reported spying on United States citizens, especially congressmen, as they traveled throughout the world almost from the time the agency was created by Congress in 1948. The USIA kept especially complete files on the trips senators and congressmen made abroad. Whether or not they were aware of the fact, members of Congress had very few private moments when they traveled abroad. In fact, President Ford was undoubtedly spied on himself, since he was a frequent world traveler when he was a congressman and since he served on the Appropriations Committee in Congress, which was a special target of the USIA. Why? Because the Appropriations Committee controlled the USIA budget, and agency members felt the secret files could be used as a way to keep the men who controlled the budget from cutting the agency's funds.

The reports themselves were a careful record of the complete overseas activities of a traveling congressman—the people he met, drank, ate, and slept with. USIA agents also kept track of how much the congressman's wife spent on clothes and gifts, and whether or not the congressman passed on or received any messages. Some members of Congress tried for years to get their files from the USIA, but their attempts were unsuccessful. Even the powerful Senate Appropriations Committee failed repeatedly. Whenever the situation became too tight for the USIA, its veteran assistant director, Ben Posner, would call for help from the Justice Department. Justice would dispatch its staff attorney, Sylvia Bacon (who later became a judge in the superior court of the District of Columbia), to argue in court and in committee councils that those files were part of "interagency" correspondence necessary to the executive branch. Therefore, the files should be withheld from the legislative branch. Today, of course, the full weight of public opinion is against suppressing such information, and new laws can be used to permit more public disclosure of such files.

It is not widely known that these secret files played a key role in the resignation of former USIA Director Edward R. Murrow. He left the job shortly after meeting with members of the Senate Appropriations Committee, who were trying so hard to get the files on themselves and other congressmen. Murrow finally agreed and promised to help. As director of the agency, Murrow really thought he should be able to release the files, but he hadn't counted on the strength and stubbornness of USIA bureaucrats. Certain of these officials refused to give up the files, and Murrow was forced to go back to Congress empty-handed. He resigned from his post a few weeks later. The public was told that Murrow resigned for reasons of health, and his health must have been failing indeed, for he died of cancer a little while later. He had been popping pills throughout the meetings. But ill health was not the only reason for Murrow's resignation from the USIA.

Whom did the USIA spy on? Whose files did they keep? Some of the USIA's best-known victims were Senator Estes Kefauver of Tennessee, Senator Dennis Chavez of New Mexico, Senator Owen Brewster of Maine, Senator John McClellan of Arkansas, Congressman Wayne Hays of Ohio (who eventually was done in by his own employee), and Congressman John Rooney of New York. Later, Rooney, who presided over the State Department's budget in the House (the State Department once had full responsibility for the USIA, and there are still ties between the two), became so cooperative with the officials in the executive branch (State and USIA) that the State Department's consular security office sent an official with Rooney to Europe. He even carried the congressman's luggage—the department considered Rooney so important to their operations.

The most notorious case of USIA watchdogging occurred when USIA employees with hidden tape recorders took down certain embarrassing remarks of Senator Allen Ellender of Louisiana. Ellender, a longtime foe of the USIA, was traveling in Africa when he was quoted as saying, "All the progress in Africa has been brought about by the whites. They put Africa on the map." The quote caused a great furor. When Ellender arrived home later, he said, "I never said that. I was misquoted." Ellender was held up to scorn and ridicule in the United States. He had always been very critical of the size of the USIA budget, and had always made detailed reports of his own on his observations of United States diplomatic personnel abroad when he returned to the Senate. Because Ellender's reports could be long and tedious, difficult for a senator to concentrate on, he tried to liven them up for his Senate colleagues by showing movies of the trip. But Ellender took his reports seriously, his facts were usually correct, and he saved money for the United States government every time he went abroad.

After his statement was made public, Ellender was made to look like a fool in such media outlets as *Time* magazine, whose editors seemed to use the USIA as if it were a subsidiary news-gathering property overseas. Therefore, when the USIA was threatened by a forthcoming Senate investigation, it was not strange that the agency called on *Time* staffers to help out by discrediting the investigators.

The investigation team, Grace Johnson and Mary Frances Holloway, two women chosen by Senator Carl Hayden, Democrat from Tempe, Arizona, then chairman of the committee, was doomed from the start. Everywhere they went on this, their second round-the-world trip, the two women were watched, whispered about, and spied upon. There was considerable jealousy among men on the committee over the fact that women had been selected. In typical USIA fashion, every fact—everything they wore, ate, drank, what time they went to bed, how loud they spoke in their hotel lobby—was noted and reported back to *Time* magazine and Senator Hayden. He received adverse reports from other staff. By the time the women returned from their investigative mission, a large number of critical dispatches had piled up on Senator Hayden's desk, and the women were fired.

The elder of the two, Mrs. Johnson, had been a highly productive employee of the Senate for thirteen years. It was Mrs. Johnson who originally suggested that the Senate committee investigating Senator Joseph McCarthy look into his tax returns. Up to then, all attempts to find legal evidence to censure McCarthy's behavior had failed. She cared so much about the security of the McCarthy files that after pretending to go home at night, she would slip back into her office and sleep next to them. Senate doors were easy to open, but not when locked from the inside. Several attempts were made to open the doors at night.

She also participated in investigations of Senate elections and had worked alongside brilliant Senator Tom Hennings of Missouri (when he was sober). Grace Johnson felt she owed her discharge to *Time* magazine, and sued them for libel. Since she was a trained investigator, she gathered evidence herself. One of her investigatory techniques was to meet USIA or State Department employees just after they returned from overseas assignments. Many a USIA agent would return to his Georgetown home and the next day find Grace Johnson and a warrant server waiting by his front door.

The depositions that came out of these encounters were full of denials—no one had ever seen Grace Johnson and companion overseas, much less spied on them, nor had people filed reports about them or sent telegrams denouncing them. Foreign service personnel swore they wouldn't know Grace Johnson if she was pointed out to them. Mrs. Johnson believed them, but this left a mystery: Who wrote the reports for the official files?

Finally, *Time* offered Mrs. Johnson a substantial settlement. A friend advised her to wait, that the court would award her even more. But Mrs. Johnson's case never came to trial.

Secrecy in Washington is rampant. The White House and the State Department set the pace. With congressional acquiescence, secrecy in the Central Intelligence Agency and the National Security Agency got completely out of control. It may be a long time before United States citizens get back their right to information about what their government is doing to them.

Secrecy is the way of life in many agencies and departments of government. Billions of dollars are spent each year at taxpayers' expense to perpetuate secrecy in government. Everything is a secret, from the multimillion-dollar cost overruns of the Defense Department construction contracts to the sale of weapons to the Shah of Iran down to a child's elementary school record marked "Confidential." Try calling any agency with a public information office and asking what that agency actually *does:* Immediately, the taxpayer gets a runaround, usually a delay, perhaps a meager explanation, finally a justification, but seldom a forthright and honest answer. Yet this is taxpayers' information that is being withheld, and the salaries of these secretive bureaucrats are paid by us, the taxpayers.

I have a suggestion for a framed wall plaque that should hang in the office of every public official from the president on down. This plaque would read: "I work for the people. They are entitled to an accounting from me. In everything I do, I must consider their interest first. Otherwise this government may cease to exist."

If there could be less secrecy, many problems in government would take care of themselves. Bureaucrats are often in the dark about what is happening in their own bureaus, and are kept from knowing much of the workings of other government agencies. If the people knew the facts, then, in the words of President Kennedy, they would be able to "make a judgment," and many problems could be resolved. It is when public officials manipulate the facts, or keep them secret, that our government doesn't work.

The post-Watergate era saw public interest centers to promote honesty, not secrecy, in government attain more clout. Ralph Nader's groups and Common Cause are among the most well known, but are certainly not the only operations of this kind. Liberals and conservatives, right wing and left, have their own organizations, funded by rich men who want to further their own causes and ideas. Some of these groups are clearly biased toward one side or the other; others have names that sound as if they had been created in the public interest. It is not widely known that many of these groups are secretly funded to promote special interests.

It is typical of the more conservative of these organizations to use the free press as a whipping boy for their own problems. Because of attacks on the media by some of these groups, and because of Vice-President Agnew's well-publicized denunciations of the press, reporters in the seventies became as unpopular as college students had been in the sixties. We had become the enemy. We were accused of being too selective in the way we reported the news; the fact that the country was in trouble was suddenly our fault. Reporters were pictured as being so powerful that we could drive a president from office. We were accused of not being "on Nixon's side." Well, we weren't. But we weren't against him, either.

Most people just do not understand that the media must act as an observer, perhaps even a critic, but never as an ally of a public officeholder. If the press is to remain free, we must broaden, not narrow, our coverage of the news. Editors and reporters have to learn that there is more happening in Washington than politicians are willing to tell us at press conferences and briefings. There is a story in the paper every day about what happened at the White House, but where are the stories about people like Mary Jones, peo-

ple who are just trying to do their job honestly, despite interference from their own government? People like Mary
must be covered, too.

We need to print more good news about real people when
it happens, and it does happen, frequently. This kind of
coverage could make people better informed about their
government, and they might understand it better and have
more respect for it. Editors must remove the straitjackets
they've put on their reporters and allow them to develop
new beats. It is up to all of us, including editors and reporters, to preserve the freedom of the press. Sometimes I
think we have self-censorship caused by limited editorial
judgment as to what to print. Senator Eugene McCarthy
was right when he said editorial judgment shuts people out.

In the mid-seventies, faced with many problems in our
own country and in the rest of the world, the American
people and the press have turned inward to examine every
aspect of American life. The Vietnam War hastened this
examination of conscience. The war taught us more than we
ever expected to know about secrecy and misdirected foreign policy. Vietnam was such a tragedy for our country
that Americans were forced to think about what our foreign
policy really meant and how it was created in the first place.
Even Henry Kissinger, foreign policy hero and winner of
the Nobel Peace Prize, became a target of public criticism.
Prodded by events and public pressure, Congress, too, began
to take back many of the powers it had either specifically
delegated or simply abdicated to the president and the secretary of state. This process will surely lead to conflict among
powerful insiders who want no controls, no participation
from Congress, and no accounting to the public for their
now traditional blank check of authority.

"Do as I say," Kissinger tried to tell the bad little boys in

Congress who dared to question Big Daddy. But the time is long past for that kind of behavior, and Congress and the American people, hungry from having been denied too long, have moved to the table. Although we haven't seen the last of government officials who prefer to operate behind closed doors, buffered from reality by blindly loyal (and ambitious) aides, President Carter has made members of his administration more accountable to the press and the public.

I am a great believer in the idea that one person, one man or woman, can significantly change things. I have seen it happen many times through the years. Am I wrong to look to the White House now for a new hero? When I think about real heroes, I think of people like Ralph Hill and Senator John Williams, who helped expose Bobby Baker's illegal activities and who made the Senate a more honest place.

Many reporters have been heroes. Drew Pearson and Jack Anderson did their best to strike fear into the hearts of public officials who had something to hide. Helene Monberg, who, like me, has run her own news bureau for years, single-handedly did more to get the crew of the *Pueblo* back home than anyone, simply by asking day after day, "What is the State Department doing now to try to get the *Pueblo* men back?" until officials were too ashamed not to act. And when I think of Daniel Schorr of CBS News giving the House committee report on CIA activities to the *Village Voice* to publish when CBS and the *Washington Post* were too scared to touch it, it reminds me of the way I used to walk around the town square in Tyler, telling everyone the story when the *Tyler Courier-Times* editors wouldn't print it.

Never underestimate the power of one man. Or of one woman. Even before two police reporters got hold of the story, a black man guarding the Watergate office building in Washington noticed that a lock was taped open on one of the doors. He notified the police, which broke open the Watergate scandal and led to imprisonment for some and the resignation of a president.

I have never forgotten that my most important role in Washington is that of a good citizen, not just reporter, although with luck, skill, and a clear head, I could be both at once. I hope I have succeeded. I have certainly tried.

I believed my role was to ask questions, and I felt that the issues which prompted those questions had a higher priority than holding back, folding my hands, and waiting for a quiet chat in a corner. Sometimes it became necessary to make noise to get an answer, like the time a Texas candidate for the Senate, Thad Hutcheson of Houston, thought it would be sharp to hold a press conference on his candidacy at the National Press Club's men's bar. That was before women were allowed to be members. The men's bar was off limits even to women guests of members. So being a woman meant that I was the only Texas reporter left out of the press conference.

I went to the club to page Hutcheson. That brought no response. He could not hear it, but I was not going to let the conference continue without my getting the news. There was no other choice left. I hammered on the club's front desk and demanded that someone go get Hutcheson. Someone did. Hutcheson came out professing innocence of club rules, apologized, and continued his press conference outside the bar with me included.

People say I am aggressive. I admit it. I believe in being aggressive. How else could a woman from east Texas get anywhere in Washington? How could any woman get anywhere in our society without being aggressive?

Some people say I've become a unique character in the

Washington press corps. I've received mail addressed to
"That Woman Reporter from Texas" or "The Woman
Who Asks Those Questions." But I still think it is important
to ask questions. For a long time, I was treated with disdain
by the male reporters and even by some of the women. But I
was not asking questions to please them.

That is all changed now. Today, most of the reporters are
friendly and polite, and they tell me I'm missed when I don't
make it to a press conference. "Where were you yesterday,
Sarah?" someone will say. "We needed some life." And once
when Secretary of State Henry Kissinger waxed long and
boring and visiting members of the American Society of
Newspaper Editors were too timid to cope with him, humor
columnist Mark Russell said out loud to a group of reporters,
"Sarah McClendon, where are you now when we need
you?"

But Washington is serious business. It is truly the news
capital of the world. Reporters can ask questions here that
may get answers which tell the future of this and other
countries. Therefore a lot of responsibility hangs on any reporter's action.

This brings me to a definition of what I think a reporter
ought to be: One who feels an obligation to the public interest to study, research, investigate, and reveal facts about
government and life. One who accompanies reporting skills
with a sense of responsibility to society and the community
around him or her, and now the world. One who seeks to
defend the downtrodden and to expose the special interests,
the special privileges that permit personal enrichment, the
special practices permitted in big business ostensibly for
profits of society but which in the long run build only more
wealth and special comforts for the very few at the expense
of the many.

Washington is really a big university where we learn major lessons every day. The successful people take advantage of the opportunity to learn. It is strictly a city of the self-made. You can do anything you are big enough to do here. But there is one thing to remember—nothing ever happens by chance.

And in a city where even the best humor is the Mark Russell kind, mixed with the issues, I will say that there are many reporters who write better than I and who are far more effective in their outlets; but I do not know anyone who gets more pleasure out of working than I do.

# Index